The Prayer Jesus Taught

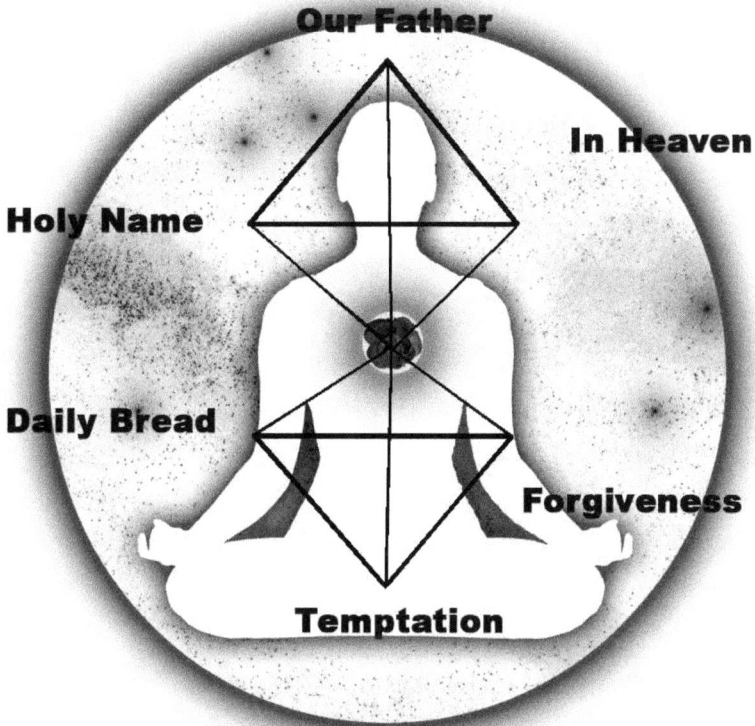

Figure 1 The Lord's Prayer

1

Cover Design by Bodie McCoy
Cover Art by Gustave Dore'
Cover Back Barbara McCoy

Published by New Genesis Inc. -
Publishing
171 Utah Mtn. Rd Waynesville NC
28785

"The Prayer Jessus Taught" by Bodie McCoy

ISBN: 978-0-9797493-4-6   e-book
ISBN: 978-0-9797493-3-9 for Print

Contents

FORWARD

THE CHRIST SEED

Twenty years of devotion and studying The Lord's Prayer have convinced Bodie and I that Jesus created His prayer to germinate, nurture and to grow the Christ Seed within us all. Like all seeds this prayer contains the blueprint of its author or parent, and within this divine blueprint we see a reflection of our truest, highest, divine Self.

Jesus clearly tells us that the "Kingdom of God is within us" and that "As we think, in our hearts we shall become." These and many other, seemingly mysterious scriptures, become clear and valuable instruction as we embrace the true purpose of The Prayer Jesus Taught.

Here Bodie offers unique perspectives and insights with spiritual exercises for opening your mind and preparing your heart as fertile soil. Take this divine seed deep into yourself. Feel it, own it as a sacred blueprint for realizing heaven on earth, and live a richly rewarding life. It's that simple.

PREFACE

Our first seven years working with The Lord's Prayer were spent in prayer, study, and contemplation. In those early years, our lives changed very quickly for the better. And it wasn't just the conditions of our lives, we also changed. During the first seven years our relationships with each other, our children, our friends, and business partners all improved significantly, as did our ability to meet and overcome our most personal challenges.

Our appreciation for The Prayer Jesus Taught , and how it had transformed our lives, inspired us to begin teaching what we had discovered about it. Since then, we've shared these insights with hundreds, perhaps even thousands of people.

While raising our large family, Barb and I lived in a very conservative small town, and this had seemed to limit our dream of reaching more people to share with. Our question has always been, how can we do this without neglecting our family?

It took a long time for us to get an answer to this question because I did not want to write a book. More than this I didn't think I could write one. In school I was a poor student and got Ds and Fs on most of my written assignments. I rarely passed a spelling test and was not a good reader. Books and writing have always been symbols of failure to me so authoring a book was the last thing I wanted to do. Well sometimes, the last thing we want is the first thing we need to do and thank God for the spell-checker. And I was quite surprised that I was able to convince a successful New York literary agent to read this book. To my utter surprise she liked it and said she knew a prominent NY editor she wanted to send it to. She told me that if the editor liked it that she had the contacts and influence to get it published.

Waiting to hear a response from her was grueling, and when it came, we found ourselves conflicted. Her response was that she thought this book would offend everyone! That was back in 2002 and now 22 years later we are optimistic that human consciousness has evolved, and many are now ready for this new way of thinking!

There are multiple benefits to saying the Lord's Prayer. And for me a big one is the freedom to share my life and myself meaningfully with others. To express myself on paper, to discipline my time, my mind and my feelings have always been exceedingly difficult but that's not what I'm doing here. I am co-creating with God to answer my own prayers and fulfill my own dreams.

It's like living in a miracle. Helping others to use this prayer, as I am, to meet your challenges and to realize your dreams enables me to share, to savor and to celebrate Our Fathers Love with you. And that is why I drafted this book originally, and why I'm sharing it with you now as humanities current spiritual awakening unfolds.

INTRODUCTION

In this book, we are introducing a new way of thinking about a prayer that you may already know. It is the most recited of all biblical scriptures and the only prayer that Jesus ever taught. It is of course "The Lord's Prayer".

Many years ago, during a personal crisis, my wife Barbara and I transformed our lives and our relationship with this prayer. Since then, as we've continued saying it daily, veiled spiritual messages and sacred symbols within it have gradually revealed themselves to us. On the surface this prayer seems to be little more than a series of prayerful requests, but going deeper we find it is much more. Hidden for the past 2000 years, ancient mystical keys within the prayer have been awaiting this time of our awakening to "The Second Coming of Christ".

Our goal here is not to merely offer a new interpretation of this prayer but to explore 26 separate ways of moving our spiritual inner awareness through it. We accomplish this in 26 short chapters, each having its own unique spiritual exercise. These chapters and exercises are progressive so each one will help to prepare you for the next. With time and practice all 26 of them may become integrated into your experience of each and every prayer.

The key to powerful prayers is our ability to take them to heart. The more we feel our prayers the more effective they become and that is the purpose of this book. So, a word of caution: The Prayer Jesus Taught is an extreme spiritual experience that changes our lives for the better. Be ready to move quickly beyond the boundaries of your current reality. Prepare to receive something better than you can imagine and be ready to let go of what you think you want, to receive something even better! This is the whole purpose of the Lord's Prayer.

We recommend that first you just read through all the chapters and their exercises. Then read them again, taking your time and allowing a full day for each chapter. For those who want to go deeper the next step is to take a full week with each chapter. And finally, to receive the maximum benefit from this book, we suggest that you learn to use it as an oracle as described on page 111.

PART I: AWAKENINGS

"Prayer enlarges the heart until it is capable of containing God's gift of Himself".

Mother Teresa

Years ago, Barbara and I attended a seminar, and afterwards a woman sitting behind us asked Barb if we were newlyweds. She laughed and told her that we'd been together twenty-four years, had eight children and seven grandchildren. The woman was amazed and asked, "how have you kept your love alive for so many years"? Barbara said, "It's being in love with God that enables us to stay in love with each other". And it is The Prayer Jesus Taught that enables and enriches our love for God.

Jesus begins his ministry saying, "Repent for the Kingdom of God is at hand". In other words, "If you will just change what you believe, (how you *be* & *live*) you will awaken to experience heaven on earth, and this is also what the Lord's Prayer says. It says, "Thy Kingdom come, *thy will* (love) be done". So, the way we experience God's kingdom on earth is through love. What the Lord's Prayer helps us to realize is that to be in love we must simply let go and let God; because God is Love, and we are created in His likeness. The experience of letting go and letting God is what we call Surfing Love, and it is simply the awakening of our own true and God-given, loving nature.

The Prayer Jesus Taught is about how Barbara and I have gradually awakened to the hidden mysteries within The

Lord's Prayer. Here we will guide you to discover a sequence of eight spiritual awakenings defining a spiritual journey to Love. You will see how this prayer can help you to stop struggling, and stressing, by simply letting go. In these first eight chapters, their spiritual exercises are opportunities to be uplifted and gently carried on the waves of Our Fathers Love. And this experience, is one of the most precious gifts of The Prayer Jesus Taught.

1. SURFING LOVE

I was born in San Diego California and raised a Catholic, but my first real church was the ocean. When I was four, I rode her waves on an air mattress, by the time I was six I could body surf, and finally when I was thirteen, I got my first surfboard. It was the ocean who taught me to ride the waves of my life. She inspired me to cultivate discipline, taught me respect, and helped me develop a strong body, and an alert mind. In her I rose above my fears, developed self-confidence, and honed my instincts. To say that surfing is a religious experience sounds cliché, but it was the ocean that taught me to honor the sacredness of each moment. She is the one who taught me that prayer is more than words. In her I learned to give every part of myself to catching the wave. And that was how I learned to pray.

Surfing the oceans waves on a great day is an awesome experience but compared to Surfing Love that experience is tame. Riding Our Fathers' Loving waves, we enter a transcendental reality that is truly not of this world. Our Father has created this wave form universe so we may learn to receive and to ride upon His many blessings. Scientifically we know the basis of everything is waves of light and sound. It's no wonder that riding His waves is how we become intimate with Our Creator and our own true selves.

The wave-like rhythms of Our Father's universe ebb and flow constantly. He is everywhere but is most accessible to us within our own breath. The sacredness of the breath was well known to the ancients and today it is still part of both Indigenous and eastern spiritual practices. The word Spirit and spiritual come from the Greek word espartos meaning to breathe. As the only activity that we do both consciously and subconsciously, breathing is a natural inner bridge between our conscious and subconscious minds. Our earthly lives begin and end with a breath. To breathe is our most immediate need and the breath of life is the unifying rhythm of all living things.

We believe the sacred breath was also something that Jesus understood and taught. He says, "Seek neither here nor there for the Kingdom of God is within you" and it is over this inner bridge, the breath, that our conscious selves travel through to our subconscious and beyond. To surf our breath, to ride it back to its' loving source, we must listen closely and surrender to its rhythms. As we pray the breathing harmonies of the life force carry us deeper into the oceans of our own consciousness. And the more fully we surrender the more completely we may know God.

I see the Lord's Prayer as a fisherman's net. Beneath the waves of our breath is a vast ocean of consciousness. As we let go, as we stop trying to control ourselves and our lives, the breath, God's cradle, gently rocks us. As we relax and let go, we sink deeper into these seas of consciousness. Our insecurities, disappointments, fears, confusion, pain, and frustrations are gently washed away. What's left is peace and love. When we let go of all our self-created realties what we find is God's reality, "Heaven".

The more we pray and gently breathe the more we let go and the more we open to receive heaven. The combined rhythms of our breath and the pure intention of our prayers enable us to relax; let go and go deeper and deeper. The more we let go the more we receive and receiving more enables us to give more. Giving more enables us to want more and the more we want the more we can let go. Jesus said, "My burden is light, and my yoke is easy" because letting go is easy and this ease is another blessing of The Prayer Jesus Taught.

BREATHING WITH THE LORD'S PRAYER

OUR (IN BREATH) FATHER (*OUT BREATH*)
WHO ART IN HEAVEN (*IN BREATH*)
HALLOWED BE THY NAME (*OUT BREATH*)
THY KINGDOM (*IN*) COME (*OUT*) THY WILL (*IN*)
BE DONE (*OUT*)
AS IT IS IN HEAVEN (*IN*) SO ALSO IN EARTH
(*OUT*)
GIVE US THIS DAY (*IN*) OUR DAILY BREAD (*OUT*)
AND FORGIVE US (*IN*) AS WE FORGIVE (*OUT*)
AND LEAD US NOT INTO TEMPTATION (*IN*) BUT
DELIVER US FROM EVIL (*OUT*)
FOR (*IN*) THYN (*OUT*) IS THE KINGDOM (*IN*)
AND THE POWER (*OUT*) AND THE GLORY (*IN*)
FOREVER (*IN*) AND EVER (*OUT*) AND EVER (*IN*)
AMEN (*OUT & IN*)

SPIRITUAL EXERCISE: The experience of surfing love begins as we let go. Imagine a wave breaking on the sand, flowing up the beach and back to the ocean. See yourself as this wave breaking and letting go completely. Now feel yourself flowing up the beach and back into the next wave or breath. Imagine this as you follow the breathing rhythms of the prayer above.

NOTES:

_____
_____
_____
_____
_____
_____
_____
_____
_____
_____
_____
_____
_____
_____
_____
_____
_____
_____

2. TURNING POINTS

Modern psychologists say our subconscious minds are like little children and that's why it's so challenging to change, control or to heal them. We believe this also explains why The Lord's Prayer can heal our human spirit. The primal rhythms of our breath and the pure intention of this prayer blend and penetrate our deepest mental and emotional barriers, touching and nurturing our inner child. This child is healed as the creative, "Spiritual Awareness of Christ, fused into this prayer, unites our conscious and sub-conscious selves. When Jesus says, "suffer these little ones come unto me," I think he meant both our outer and our inner children. And when he says, "lest ye become as little children you may not enter the Kingdom of heaven," I believe he's telling us that our inner child is an important key to our spiritual growth.

When reciting The Lord's Prayer, it begins by proclaiming ourselves as Gods children , saying, "Our Father." And it is my own inner child that I want to share with you now. On a cool February afternoon in 1953 my grandmother took me to see the Disney movie Peter Pan. It was my fourth birthday, and that afternoon Peter gave me the greatest gift a four-year-old could receive. He invited us, the audience, to stand and take an oath. And by the way he spoke, I knew it was sacred. It was an oath "to never grow up". As Peter spoke, I thought about how my own parents didn't seem very happy and didn't seem to have much fun. That is why I eagerly took his oath. A few months later I saw my first surfer flying across the waves just like Peter Pan flew across the sky. The oath had already begun shaping my destiny.

When I started school, about a year later, my teachers never had a chance. School was about growing up and my teachers, like Captain Hook, seemed intent on sucking the fun out of my life. School was like in the movie; they were always trying to catch me. They wanted me to walk their plank, but I always got away, or so I thought. When I was 13, I discovered a tribe of Pans, called surfers.

The 60's were like heaven to me, dancing on the waves and searching for Never-Never Land. Then, in Hawaii, just when I thought I'd found it, on a warm evening in 1970 I flew too high on several tabs of LSD. Terrified I reached out to a long-forgotten God, and He reached back and touched me.

After that I was still a Pan looking for Never-Never Land. And in fact, my quest was renewed. But now I was looking within myself, where God had touched me. Like many other lost boys, I moved to Los Angeles where a spiritual and psychological renaissance was underway. Over the next seven years I explored eastern disciplines like meditation, yoga and Tai Chi and several western "therapies" like Primal Scream, Richen Breath Work, Gestalt and Bioenergetics.

During those years I learned about herbs and became a vegetarian. I dabbled with oracles like the I Ching, Tarot and astrology and I studied with gurus, healers, and teachers. But during those seven long years I gradually forgot what I was looking for.

In Los Angeles, I supported myself as a waiter working in the finest restaurants and country clubs. There, in my disguise, I was serving the real Captain Hooks, but they were too self-absorbed to notice. I had a fun, carefree adventurous life that Peter would have been proud of, but he was about the only one. I honored my promise "to never grow up" but as I got older keeping that promise became harder. Then finally one day in 1976 I suddenly was overwhelmed with a sense that life was passing me by. I was 27 and everyone I knew seemed to be making lots of money and building families. Feeling left out and fearing the dreaded "I told you so", I decided to become an inventor. It was a simple plan, a Peter Plan; I would invent something, sell it for a lot of money and rub all "their" noses in my success.

To the amazement of everyone, except Peter, my first invention, a sports game, was a success. The buyer at Sears loved it and while I sat there in his office, he called a manufacturer in Texas. He told his manufacturer he wanted my game ASAP and when I left his office that morning he asked if I had any idea how rare it was for something like that to happen. I didn't know, but two days later, when I was in Dallas negotiating a royalty agreement with the manufacturer, I was asked the very same question. Over the next few years, I learned about business and patience but mostly patience.

In July of 1977 I met my wife, Barbara. It was love at first sight but as Peter would tell you, when a Pan falls in love things can get pretty messy! It's hard to be a kid with a wife and children of your own. And three years after meeting Barbara we had four children. Hers, mine, and ours! I was in shock, but my never-ending deal with Sears was finally about to pay off. Or so I thought. A sequence of bazaar events caused Sears to back out of our deal, but I rebounded and went on to invent "The Total Trainer". When 'The Trainer' met with a similar fate the Pan in me, feeling trapped and exhausted, fell to his knees and prayed.

In those days, my prayers were mostly acts of desperation. The events that had prevented my success were not normal, and there was even a sense that God Himself was holding me back. Feeling confused, I asked Him what I'd done wrong? And a clear, gentle inner voice said, "You cannot succeed this way". To the Pan in me this seemed incredibly unfair, but I also knew there was something else I was supposed to be doing with my life.

I'd known this since I was a young child, but what was it? Feeling confused and exhausted I fell into a deep sleep, and I awoke hearing that same gentle inner voice asking me, "what do you want"? Without thinking I said, "I just want to be a good father". Then the voice asked, "what did you want from your father"? Again, without thinking I heard, "permission to follow my heart". "How could he give you that", the voice asked? By following his own. Then there was a long silence.

My whole life up to that moment, surfing, Hawaii, moving to LA, becoming an inventor, meeting Barbara, and becoming a father, had been affected by my inner child's oath "to never grow up". I'd been living in two separate realities. There was my child's quest to find Never-Never Land and my adult self who had to survive in "The Real World". The Lord's Prayer brings these two realities together to heal our soul. We are God's children, young and old alike. To be our true selves we must transcend the conditions of our hearts, our minds, and the world we live in. This prayer helps us do this.

TURNING POINT CHOICES
(Choices in the prayer)

OUR: Our first choice is to live as God's child.

OUR: Our second choice is to love and embrace God's family.

FATHER: To accept Our Fathers grace, protection, and authority.

WHO ART IN HEAVEN: To seek perfection within ourselves.

HALLOWED BE THY NAME: To honor our own words as sacred.

THY KINGDOM COME: To make heaven on earth our #1 goal.

THY WILL BE DONE: To always use love; in all ways.

AS IN HEAVEN: To look for the goodness in everything & everyone.

GIVE US THIS DAY: To receive and consume this day.

AND FORGIVE US AS WE FORGIVE: To forgive, no matter what.

AND LEAD US NOT INTO TEMPTATION: To seek only God.
DELIVER US FROM EVIL or ILLUSION: Let go and let God.
FOR THYN IS THE KINGDOM THE POWER & THE GLORY FOREVER AMEN: To embrace God as all that we desire!

SPIRITUAL EXERCISE: With every new choice our lives flow in new ways and directions. So, what is stopping you from making the choices you really want? Ask yourself, what if you had all the money and everything else that you could possibly want or need, what would you choose"? Who would you be? What would you do? As you recite The Lord's Prayer, reflect on each of its choices. Observe how these choices affect you. Know that your willingness to let go and choose "His Will" determines your reality.

NOTES:

_____
_____
_____
_____
_____
_____
_____
_____
_____

3. AS A CHILD

That evening, as I spoke with this gentle inner voice, every question and every answer helped me to let go. My years of hard work, my dreams and thousands of dollars were all gone and there was really nothing I could do about that. There wasn't anyone to fight with or anything to fight for. It was all gone. When the voice asked what I wanted I said, "to be a good father," something within me let go. Two days earlier I would have said something like success or money, but beneath those desires there was always that one, and I could no longer afford to place those conditions on my truth.

When I said that I wanted to be a good father I was also admitting that I didn't feel like I was one, and that was exceedingly difficult. When the voice asked what I wanted from my father I heard; "Permission to follow my heart". I had to accept the painful reality of never having been trusted that much. When the voice asked, "How could he have given you that" it was clear "By his example, by following his own heart." I also had to realize that my father had not trusted himself enough to do that, and this too was painful. The truth hurt because I had been living a lie. Seeing money as the solution to my problems was safe compared to looking at what I really needed to be happy.

As that lie came to an end more old feelings came to the surface. There was a lot I had to let go of before the truth could set me free. I remembered how my parents had wanted me to become a doctor and what a poor student I'd been. Deep within me my inner child believed he had not been a good son so how could he hope to be a good father? I'd been hauling around these conflicts most of my life and letting them go felt very liberating. For the first time in a long while I felt grateful. Not for anything special, just to be alive and to not be a doctor! My parents' expectations had strengthened me, but until I let go of my self judgements and the memories of our battles over my choices, I couldn't put my strengths to good use.

To be a good father I had to follow my own heart. We'd come full circle, but this time when my gentle inner voice asked again, "what do you want", I was amazed. My mind was blank. I couldn't imagine that kind of freedom. There was another long silence before the voice asked me, "when can you remember being really happy and excited about your life?"

Before I could even give it much thought, I saw my seven-year-old self, studying for my first communion being fascinated with the Lords' Prayer. For some reason I believed it was "magical." And if I said it "right" I would see God, and that my life would become magical too. Where did I get this idea? I don't really know, no one did. I remember how confused and concerned my mother was to see me praying every night. It wasn't like me, and the nuns who taught me in catechism were also surprised.

Then late one night I heard my parents fighting. They were both yelling, and this was unusual. Apparently, Monsignor Ott, our pastor, had called that day and told my mother that my "obsession" with the prayer was "unhealthy and even blasphemous." He said he thought I needed "professional help." Now Mom and Dad were fighting because Dad, who wasn't Catholic, didn't care what the monsieur thought, and Mom was afraid for my soul, and hers.

As I continued listening to them, I was grateful for my dad's stubbornness. I didn't know what a "shrink" was, but it didn't sound particularly good. That evening my relationship to my parents, to The Church, to Jesus and the innocent child who believed in the magic of The Lord's Prayer all got shrouded in doubt and buried deep in me.

Now, many years later, I was amazed to see how the child in me was still waiting and believing. I was deeply touched by his faith, and I yearned for his innocence and dreams. Without thinking I reached out to that wounded child in me and promised to rejoin his quest to discover the "magic" of the Lord's Prayer. Quickly, my cynical voices rose up in my head to criticize and judge me, but I knew, to be a good father, I had to follow my own inner child's dream. Later that evening I told Barbara about my experience. First, she said she could see a change in me. And then she laughed because when she was about seven, she'd had a remarkably similar experience while reciting the Lord's Prayer. Since that evening, we've pursued the "magic" of this prayer together and our journey has indeed been truly magical.

SPIRITUAL EXERCISE: The Lord's Prayer begins with "Our Father" to emphasize that we are God's children. It's our innocence that enables us to receive the magical and miraculous reality of Our Father's Kingdom.

Every child needs to feel loved so when do you remember needing to feel loved? Who or what do you believe could have given you what you needed? How? You may not still want the same thing, but the child within you still wants that same feeling. Before you begin to pray say "Father, this is what I want(this feeling), and Thy will be done". Letting go to receive it or something better for the Highest Good. As you do this observe how you feel and pray with that feeling.

NOTES:_____

_____
_____
_____
_____
_____
_____
_____
_____
_____
_____
_____
_____
_____
_____
_____
_____
_____

4. VULNERABLITY+HUMILITY

When I look back at the major turning points of my life, I see some common threads. Each significant life change has been preceded by an experience of conflict or difficulty. Next, I felt vulnerable and then humbled. Then each time I said some kind of prayer and from that prayer came my willingness to make a new choice. Finally, something miraculous would happen effortlessly and magically that changed my life completely. When I say miraculous, I mean that something happened that without making any real effort would happen to fulfill my prayer in a way that was better than I could have imagined.

I now see how each of these miracles began to unfold when I went out into the raging storm of my life where I was thrashed by its unrideable waves. Eventually the fighting, struggling and hard work wore me out and I had to let go. Feeling defeated I let go even more and this is when I was carried into the eye of my storm. There, with nothing else to do, I prayed, opened my heart, and soon the magic began to happen. Each time I let go after that, my life changed quickly and easily for the better. I now realize that this is exactly what the Lord's Prayer helps me to do without all the drama. The freedom this prayer gives me to let go allows me to change and move more quickly and efficiently through my life.

For the most part we humans do seem to require conflict before we are willing to let go and let God. For example, the day after 9/1/01 I spent most of the day watching more news coverage of the World Trade Center and Pentagon tragedies. As I watched I observed my disbelief. I knew it was real, but I felt numb, and helpless, and then I began to pray. A terrible act of cruelty had just been perpetrated. Thousands of people were dying, and suffering and my prayers didn't change any of that. However, they liberated me to experience this "tragedy" as a profound opportunity.

I was praying for those who were dead, dying, suffering and afraid when I heard my inner voice say, "It's the terrorist who really need your prayers". So, I began reciting The Lord's Prayer and praying for the ones who had done this terrible thing, I suddenly felt very vulnerable. I could feel myself wanting them to suffer, and then I came to the part of the prayer that says, "Forgive us our trespasses as we forgive those who trespass against us." In forgiveness, I felt naked and vulnerable, but as I began to say the prayer again, I could feel it more deeply than before. I looked at my life and I saw how my most magical experiences came when I was feeling the most vulnerable.

Vulnerability is living with prayer as our only protection. It is putting our faith in Our Fathers power and glory when we cannot see how, when, or why. To receive God's will, we must let go of our own. That is how we sacrifice our human heart on the altar of our lives. This is the choice each of us lives with every day; "do we become defensive? Do we run, hide, or fight? Or do we say, "Lord this is what I want, but Thy will be done." Do we cover our vulnerability as Adam and Eve did? Do we hide from God, or do we stand naked before Him in prayer?

Jesus said, "I in and of myself can do nothing" and there's really nothing any of us can really do effectively until we pray. Prayer creates the space for Our Fathers will, which is love, to enter our hearts. Then we know what we are to do, and it doesn't need to make sense because we just know.

Jesus was both vulnerable and humble! He was an "illegitimate child", born in a barn with a price on his head. He worked as a humble carpenter and in the end, he was beaten, mocked, spit on and crucified. He bled to death in front of his friends and family and afterwards some even denied ever knowing him. And here's the kicker; His is the ultimate success story because vulnerability + humility + prayer = miracles. Jesus didn't run, hide, or fight. He humbly prayed, "Father, thy will be done" and "Forgive them for they know not what they do". His life, like the prayer he taught, is an example of how vulnerability + humility + prayer = miracles i.e. His ascension.

When I was a child, my parents wanted the best for me and for them that meant getting a good education. Right from the beginning I did poorly in school, so they had me evaluated. The tests said I was actually pretty smart, so they tested me again. When the second test said the same thing, they assumed I just wasn't trying. Being committed to my oath to never grow up and unable to please them I felt very vulnerable. Back then having lots of energy my vulnerability just made me fight them harder, and the harder I fought the harder they fought, and by the time I was in high school we had a rather ugly war going.

My worst subject in school was always English. I got Ds and Fs on most written assignments and here I am writing a book which is a lot like those assignments. Sending this manuscript to a publisher is also a lot like passingit in to be graded. All those years of not doing well in school are still a part of who I am today. All our experiences when we are young become a part of who we are, and that doesn't change much, except our relationship with them. So, what I am doing here also makes me feel very vulnerable, and I can't change that, but now I don't even want to.

The Lord's Prayer has helped me learn how even my greatest fears and weaknesses can become my greatest strengths. To have a happy and magical life, maintaining with integrity my oath to never grow up as I remember I am always a child of God, keeps me in a constant state of letting go and vulnerability, which enables me to pray and experience the miracle of authoring this book and sharing my heart.

SPIRITUAL EXERCISE: To use this formula, vulnerability + humility + prayer = miracles we begin by allowing ourselves to care deeply. So, what do you care most about? If you had no limitations, how would you honor your caring? What would you create? It takes courage to own what we really want and more courage to make it our top priority. "Seeking the Kingdom first" (happiness) is for those with brave hearts.

The Lord's Prayer is for creating heaven on earth but first we must have an extraordinary, heavenly dream and the courage to commit ourselves to it. And dreams begin with feelings, so if that's all you're aware of that's all you need to begin realizing your true co-creative relationship with God. Again, before you begin your prayer say, "Lord this is what I care about, and this is what I want, and Thy will be done". As you surrender your desires to God, feel yourself letting go and know that your sacrifice will be returned to you both amplified and perfected. In other words, open your heart and mind to receive something much, much better than you ever imagined.

NOTES:_____

_____
_____
_____
_____
_____
_____
_____
_____
_____
_____
_____
_____
_____
_____
_____
_____
_____
_____

5. CREATIVE RESPONSIBILITY

When Barbara and I began pursuing the magic of the Lord's Prayer, oh so many years ago, we were led to Mathew 6: where, in the "Sermon on the mount", Jesus prepares us to receive his prayer. First, he says: "When you pray go into your closet, and when you have shut the door, pray to your Father which is in secret; and your Father who is in secret shall reward you openly". As usual what he says is "for those with eyes to see and ears to hear" and what we see and hear is the instruction to go into the silence within ourselves, where God is. And we shall be rewarded openly in our daily lives. What Jesus is describing here is how to pray by entering a deep and receptive, meditative state of mind.

Next Jesus says: "when you pray do not use vain repetitions, as the heathen do; for they think they shall be heard for their much speaking." In this we hear him telling us that it's not the quantity of our words but the quality of our feelings and intentions that determines the effectiveness of our prayers. And this is also what vulnerability + humility + prayer = miracles is about. Being vulnerable, like a child, brings our deepest feelings and intentions into our prayers and this is what makes them effective.

Finally, Jesus says: "Your Father knows what things you have need of before you ask him. After this manner therefore pray: Our Father who is in heaven, holy is thy name...." This part seems like a riddle because if our prayers are not to inform God of our needs then what are they for? If it's not a request, then what's "Give us this day our daily bread" about? The answer is quite simple. We are "gods" and as creators-in-training we must accept, consume, and learn from our creations one day at a time.

This is also why we ask for forgiveness. We take from this day what we can consume, digest, and assimilate. The rest is the waste we let go of through forgiveness. And again, the prayer affirms The Creator's law "As we give (forgive) so shall we receive (forgiveness)". Those who need to may think of this prayer as a request, but it's actually an extremely specific blueprint to help us build our own unique heaven here on earth.

God is life, and life is hungry, so we pray "And lead us not into temptation   but deliver us from evil". By the way, "evil" is "live" backwards. God is both the essence of hunger and the sweetness, beauty, power, glory, and goodness that we hunger for. Our external relationships distract us from "Seeking the Kingdom of God within ourselves". We can see, hear, smell, touch and taste the external goodness, but these sensations are illusions of life, not the real thing. These outer illusions are what the bible calls false gods, filling us with both false promises and fears until we let them go. The law of balance (the attraction of opposites) compels us to vacillate between our wants and fears. Our fears cancel our wants, and our wants cancel our fears, and this is how God's law prevents us from moving too far or fast in the wrong direction. By saying "Lord this is what I want, and Thy will (love) be done" we release our limited sensory desires, our false gods, our illusions of life. This is how Our Fathers love delivers us from evil.

SPIRITUAL EXERCISE: As you begin to pray go within yourself and direct your words to God who is within you. Think of something that you want or something you are afraid of. Now say "Lord this is what I want, or this is what I do not want and "Thy will be done". Feel yourself letting go of what you want to receive something better. As you pray be aware that giving what you desire to God is the best possible way of opening to receive a true miracle. Feel God's love flowing into and through you and back out into the world. See His love lifting and blessing your whole life and everyone in it.

NOTES;_____
_____
_____
_____
_____
_____
_____
_____
_____

6. HALLOWED BE THY NAME

It is believed that through sacred tones man may reach a higher consciousness and that certain elements of his nature may even be changed. In the East sacred words, called mantras, are believed to vibrate in harmony with Our Creator. In Hebrew, for example, Yahweh is a "Sacred Name of God" and the word Om, expressing the essence of the supreme Absolute, consciousness," is a sacred mantra revered by the Hindus. It is believed that by chanting and meditating on these "Sacred Names of God" with reverence and devotion we may attain God consciousness through our surrender to His presence within us. This also describes what I felt about the Lord's Prayer when I was seven.

Our experiences of worshiping God both through Eastern meditations and the Lord's Prayer make us believe that when Jesus says, "Hallowed be Thy Name", in the Lord's Prayer, he's directing us to God's resonance or sound within ourselves. To our Western minds this may sound odd but it's only because we're used to pursuing external goals. The word holy means "worthy of worship" and worshiping God's "Holy Name" is for those who are ready to become truly intimate with Our Creator.

Eastern spiritual teachers describe a holy river, a "Sacred Sound Current" emanating from God's Heart, loving, and sustaining all of creation. Again, this may sound strange yet when Jesus says, "Man does not live by bread alone but by every word from the mouth of God" he's saying the same thing. In Genesis we find "In the beginning was

The Word and The Word was with God and The Word was God" so all of creation must have come from this "Word". Today when our modern scientists explore beneath the atomic and subatomic levels guess what they find? An illusive sound that seems to be coming from everywhere. The agreements of Eastern and Western religions with modern science reveal to us what "Hallowed be Thy name" is really about.

Barbara and I believe this mysterious sound is both the biblical "Word" and "God's Holy Name". We believe that in the Lord's Prayer, Jesus introduces us to a "Western mantra" which has the ability to quicken our spiritual growth through intimacy with God. And we believe he intended that we would understand it's true significance at this very moment.

In the East, faith (religion) precedes understanding (science). In the West, it's just the opposite so our technological growth is faster than our spiritual ability to cope with it. We see The Lord's Prayer as our "Fathers" secret weapon. And we believe that Jesus gave us this prayer so that we could evolve quickly before we destroy ourselves.

SPIRITUAL EXERCISE: The world we live in is alive with sound, with "The Word" who is Our Creator. It is everywhere and in everything but to know it we must go within and listen carefully. Listen to your breath and through your breath. You may hear the "sound current" as running water or thundering surf but whether you hear it right away or not, directing your prayers to this Sacred Word will carry you deeper into Gods Heart. To hear God's name, we listen where it is, and it is everywhere. Listening in every direction at once we enter a neutral state of mind where we may feel and hear God's Holy Spirit responding to our intention. Be patient and know The Lord is always with you in every moment and in every breath.

NOTES:_____

_____
_____
_____
_____
_____
_____
_____
_____
_____
_____
_____
_____
_____
_____
_____
_____
_____
_____
_____

7. DIVINE ATTUNEMENTS

One afternoon, in my favorite bookstore, I found two old books on the Lord's Prayer. Both described the prayer as a progression of seven "divine attunements". While contemplating these my gentle inner voice suggested there might be a connection between these attunements and the body's seven chakras, or energy centers. This connection was surprisingly easy to see and over the next few weeks I experimented with how the prayer and the chakras could be combined with eastern yoga and meditation techniques. The image on the following page will be helpful in helping you too see what I see.

(See fig. on next page)

1. CROWN CHOKRA
OUR
FATHER

The crown is
our identity as
Gods Children.

The Third Eye
in Eastern
spiritual
teachings often
refer to this
center as the
window to
heaven.

2. THIRD EYE
WHO ART IN HEAVEN

3. THROAT
HALLOWED BE THY NAME

The Throat
Chakra falls over
the voice box.

Gods will is love,
and as we open
our hearts to one
another we create
heaven on earth.

4. HEART
Thy Kingdom Come thy will be done.

5. SOLAR PLEXUS:
GIVE US THIS DAY OUR DAILY BREAD:
Falls over the
"Breadbasket"

6. NAVEL:
FORGIVE US OUR ERRORS AS WE FORGIVE OTHERS:
Forgiveness is part of digestion.
What we can't assimilate is the waste we let go

7. SEXUAL CENTER or BASE CHOKRA
LEAD US NOT INTO TEMPTATION BUT DELIVER US FROM EVIL:
We're tempted by the goodness our senses perceive, but evil
(live spelled backwards) is just a reflection, ("the Kingdom
of God is within us").

As you can see there is a direct and obvious correlation between these seven attunements and our seven chakras. Barbara and I knew these chakras, or energy centers, were central to the spiritual teachings of the Far East and seeing how they were also present in the Lord's Prayer made us feel that Jesus, as many believe, may have studied in the Far East. It is possible that eastern masters taught Jesus this prayer or it may have come through him directly from the Christ. Either way there's a definite connection between The Prayer Jesus Taught and the spiritual disciplines of the Far East.

By praying while focusing our attention and breath into these chakras we were quickly moved into deeper meditative states than before. We experienced God's Holy Name more quickly and easily than before. Praying this way took us deep into the "sound current". Our spiritual awareness was enhanced, and our spirits were lifted. And riding the sound current of life in this way was physically, mentally, and emotionally healing and invigorating.

It was also rewarding that our years of practicing Eastern Meditations were enhancing our relationship to Jesus through The Prayer He Taught. If you'vehad previous experiences with meditation by now you may realize what a wonderful and unique meditation The Lord's Prayer is. If not, then this will be the beginning of a whole new experience for you.

It is especially rewarding for us when we hear that praying this way provides the first really deep, healing spiritual experience that some of our students have ever had. This also makes sense to us because The Prayer Jesus Taught is obviously a spiritual exercise specifically crafted to serve the specific spiritual needs of our modern western culture.

SPIRITUAL EXERCISE: Familiarize yourself with the correlations between these seven attunements in the prayer and the chakras (see fig.). As you pray move your awareness and your breath through these seven centers. Imagine that you are actually breathing in and out through each chakra. As you pray consciously relax and let go of any tension in each of these centers. Using the wave breath (Ch #1) and listening (Ch #6) will help you to go deeper and to have a fuller and more rewarding experience.

NOTES:

_____
_____
_____
_____
_____
_____
_____
_____
_____
_____
_____
_____
_____
_____

8. PROMISES

"As you think, in your heart you shall become."

In our modern world the closest thing to a sacred word is a promise and that's really what a prayer is. The power of a prayer is determined by the depth of our feelings plus the sincerity and purity of our intention. When we take a prayer to heart, we honor it as sacred and imbue it with our God-given life force. It's our own sacred words that empower us to create and it is "vain repetitions" that weaken our creative force. In prayer we look within to know the meaning and purpose of our lives because this, above all, is what our prayers help us to fulfill.

Fortunately, we are God's children and yet our fears, defensiveness and outwardly motivated lives may harden our hearts, and this is why Jesus taught this prayer. The spiritual promise that it holds ignites and enlivens our spirits with the hope that we may fulfill the dream of our soul. When I was seven, I perceived its promise as: "If you say this prayer right you will experience God and your life will become magical". By the time I was 33 I'd forgotten it and had become very cynical but there was still part of me that remembered. There is a hopeful child within us all who remembers, and this is whom our prayers are really for.

Soon after rededicating my life to this prayer, I realized that to receive its promise I must give my own promise. The magic of this prayer, like the primal wave rhythms of life, begins with receiving and giving. As we receive Christ's promise and give our own, we enter into an accelerated, "magical", creative cycle, because God always gives us more. To Barbara and me the Lord's Prayer is like a creators' blueprint. To live as "gods", we require a superior code of ethics and the Lord's Prayer provides one in the form of sixteen sacred promises.

THE SIXTEEN PROMISES

OUR FATHER (CROWN):
*CHRIST'S PROMISE; as God's children we are perfectly loved, cared forand protected at all times.
*OUR PROMISE; is to receive God's blessings and to love all His
children as our spiritual family.
WHO ART IN HEAVEN (THIRD EYE):
*CHRIST'S PROMISE: The Kingdom of God is within you".
*OUR PROMISE; to seek first His inner Kingdom.
HALLOWED BE THY NAME (THROAT):
*CHRIST'S PROMISE; the more we listen to The Word/His voice, the more sacred, holy, and loving our own thoughts and lives will become.
*OUR PROMISE; is to listen, speak and think of Him.
THY KINGDOM COME THY WILL BE DONE AS IT IS INHEAVEN SO ALSO IN EARTH (HEART):
*CHRIST'S PROMISE; Our Fathers Kingdom will come as we love.
*OUR PROMISE; to love ourselves, our neighbors, even our enemies.

GIVE US THIS DAY OUR DAILY BREAD (SOLAR PLEXUS):
*CHRIST'S PROMISE; is that all we need is perfectly provided.
*OUR PROMISE; is to accept and honor the perfection of our lives.
FORGIVE US AS WE FORGIVE (NAVEL):
*CHRIST'S PROMISE; to error is part a growth process.
*OUR PROMISE; to learn from our errors and let others do the same.
LEAD US NOT INTO TEMPTATION BUT DELIVER US FROM EVIL (BASE/SEXUAL)
*CHRIST'S PROMISE; as we let go, we're delivered from our illusions.
*OUR PROMISE; is to let go so we may receive His blessings.
FOR THYN IS THE KINGDOM AND THE POWER AND THE GLORY FOR EVER AND EVER
(IN ALL CENTERS)
*CHRIST'S PROMISE; all that we could ever want is already within us.
*OUR PROMISE; to receive all that Our Father is and to give our praise and all that we are so that we may receive and give more and more.

Our ability to receive, to give and create in our human lives evolves with our ability to receive and to give these promises. We enter into a sacred covenant with Christ as we perceive and honor the promises in this prayer first within our hearts and then in our daily lives. Reflect on your ability to give and to receive these promises. Observe how each promise is an opportunity to grow and to prosper spiritually, mentally, emotionally, physically.

Amen: We conclude our prayers with the word Amen, which we generally think of as meaning "The End". A more accurate translation would be "Sealed in truth". Saying Amen (sealed in truth) confirms that the Lord's Prayer is an oath given with our sacred word or promise. Christ comes into our hearts and our lives as we honor His promise as Jesus did. The more we honor this oath as sacred the more we may receive Our Father's Love and the more magically The Lord's Prayer can touch and affect our daily lives.

SPIRITUAL EXERCISE: As you say this prayer, move your attention and breathe through your chakras. Feel how willing you are to receive and to give in each of these centers. Where do you feel most open? Where do you feel resistance or doubt? What does this tell you about yourself? Intend now that your heart and mind become willing vessels of Our Father's Love. Know that you are Gods child, a divine creator. Feel the honor, the power, and the glory of your divine heritage. As you pray feel His creative force growing within you. See and feel yourself radiating with love as you receive His promise.

PART II : ILLUSIONS

As God's children we are perfectly loved and cared for at all times. This is the first and primary promise of the Lord's Prayer but after a tragedy like an earthquake or a terrorist attack we may wonder if God really does love us or if He even exists. And if there is a God, where was he on 9-11-01? We believe He was sending us all a 911 emergency call. God didn't fly those planes, but He did give us free will. His love is always present as promised, but to receive His love we must learn to choose wisely and to honor our own promise to love one another.

In that dark moment as the Twin Towers, symbols of duality, commerce, money, and power, were being destroyed we heard God saying, "it's time to stop worshiping our false god" ($). When the Pentagon was struck, we heard Him say, "might does not make right". And when the White House, a symbol of America's free will was spared, we heard "I will honor your choices". If we see these events as opportunities to grow and to love, then those who lost their lives will have blessed us all. And we heard the words, "Father, forgive them for they know not what they do."

God has been gentle and patient with us but recently our creative potential has grown very rapidly. This means we must also accept greater creative responsibility. Until we got that 911 call most of us thought things were pretty ok, but warring and competing for power and money is not in harmony with Our Fathers will. We have seen more compassion and love since September 11th, but we've also heard a lot of accusations, and as usual little acceptance of responsibility. This is a wake-up call. Either we start living as one loving and responsible human family or we will surely get more wake-up calls. Exposing and seeing through the illusions that keep us separate is what both the Lord's Prayer and this section of this book are all about.

NOTES:_____

_____
_____
_____
_____
_____
_____
_____
_____
_____
_____
_____
_____
_____
_____
_____
_____
_____
_____
_____
_____

9. OUR FATHER

None of us come from perfect homes so it's important for us to realize how our relationships with our families affect our relationship with God. Growing up my mother and father were very restrictive and controlling and that is also how I felt about God. Do you think that's a coincidence? It's not. As babies and young children our parents are our gods. We are completely dependent on them for everything so everything about them affects us. And later in life we all tend to project their strengths, weaknesses, and personalities on God.

Walt Whitman once said, "My religion is expressed in the first two words of the Lord's Prayer". He is Our Father; we are His children, and we are His family. If we could honor these first two words in the prayer, we would live full, happy & productive and spiritual lives. But to do this we must let go of all that we have ever known. God transcends even our most creative imaginations. He is "The Alpha and Omega, the beginning, and the end". He is the great circle of life encompassing every atom, planet, solar system, galaxy, and every soul. Everything and everyone rotates around its true center, and He is that center.

By creating false centers, or gods, we create imbalance and the naturally spiraling, spiritual motion of our spirits must rotate slower. Thus, our minds, emotions, our bodies, and our lives become denser. This is what makes us susceptible to both illusions and disease. Focusing away from our true center we become trapped in our own illusions. We come from Our Father, and our destiny is to return to Him. He is Love and Love is our ultimate desire. To release our false gods and fulfill our destiny we must literally reprogram our hearts and minds, and this is exactly what the Lord's Prayer helps us do. *In essence, the Lord's Prayer is a spiritual journey beginning with God and returning to God while passing through every dimension of our human experience.*

There are two different versions of the Lord's Prayer in the bible. In Luke 11: the prayer ends with the seventh attunement, ("Lead us not into temptation but deliver us from evil, Amen"). In Matthew 6: however, there's an eighth attunement, ("For Thyn is the kingdom and the power and the glory forever, Amen"). There's long been a debate as to whether this eighth attunement was part of the original prayer and at one point Barb and I felt it didn't fit with the pattern of the chakras. Now, however, we see how it does and this eighth attunement also beautifully completes the circle of our lives.

Jesus says, "The first shall be last and the last first" and this final attunement beautifully brings us back to the prayers first two words. In those first two words we are young children. Then the prayer takes us on a journey through the concerns of our daily bread, forgiveness, and temptation.

Then we arrive at the eighth attunement as Our Fathers adult children. And this final attunement addresses our adult desires for a kingdom, for power, glory and even eternity. These are the domains of Our Father, and they beautifully correspond with our seven chakras. Jesus says, "I and my Father are one" and this is also what we are saying in this final attunement. We experience "falling in love" as "losing control" and our surfing journey within, to God's Kingdom, also feels a lot like falling. Our human will is focused through our senses outward so the only way into His Kingdom is by letting go. The first seven attunements of the prayer prepare us, and this final attunement is our total surrender. We literally ignite our chakra centers as we say in surrender, "For Thyn is the Kingdom and the power and the glory forever and ever and ever Amen".

CROWN
* FOR THYN; Our Father;
THIRD EYE
* IS THE KINGDOM; In Heaven;
THROAT
*THE POWER; Hallowed be thy name;
HEART
*AND THE GLORY; Thy Will/Love;
SOLAR PLEXUS
*FOREVER: Give us this day;
NAVEL
*AND EVER: Forgive us;
SEXUAL
*AND EVER; Lead us not into temptation;
*AMEN;

SPIRITUAL EXERCISE: Say this final attunement moving your attention and breathe through the appropriate chakras. Feel the radiance of Gods power and glory igniting each center. Feel your life force building. Do this and observe how your challenges and fears just melt away.

NOTES:

_____
_____
_____
_____
_____
_____
_____
_____
_____
_____
_____
_____
_____
_____
_____
_____
_____
_____
_____
_____
_____

10. OUR MOTHER

People often assume that our ministry is primarily the result of my work but that's not true. Yes, I do most of the writing, lecturing and the actual creative work but without Barbara I would not be able to do these things. Barbara's role is equal to mine, yet people have a tough time seeing this because her part is more subtle. And in general, we humans have valued the active male role more than the passive female. But the truth is both male and female aspects exist within each of us. Our feminine self possesses our receptivity, so by diminishing her we impede our ability to receive, to give, and to love.

When Barbara and I first met naturally we hoped to have a wonderful life together, but it didn't take long for our own prejudice to start undermining our dreams. Like my father I saw our home as a ship, and as the man I believed I should be the captain. It wasn't an ego trip or even what I really wanted. I was just trying to be a good husband and father. Barbara, being true to herself, felt she was supposed to be more than my first mate. Now I agree with her but at the time our male egos fought for what each of us believed was right, and this put a great strain on our relationship and our family.

Living in fear of a mutiny and horrified to see myself turning into Captain Hook, I felt my dreams slowly melting away. I didn't have a clue what to do. Our society and even the bible seems to affirm male superiority, especially in a marriage. In Eph. 5: 23 Paul says, "For the husband is the head of the wife as Christ is the head of the Church". In Gen. 3: 16 God says to Eve "you shall be dependent on your husband, and he shall rule over you". When we isolate these scriptures the picture we see is distorted because like our lives, and Our Fathers universe, the bible is a whole and very big picture.

We believe the bibles pure intent here is first to introduce us to the captain of our souls, and secondly to deliver us from the false twisted "Might Makes Right" authority of our male egos. The bible has survived the corrupt male authority of Popes, crusaders, evangelists, and scribes for thousands of years, not because of its many words, but because of its' pure and incorruptible intent. It's affected our lives more than any other human creation and yet it is only holy if and when it is used to serve the highest good of our sacred and God given souls.

Before we rediscovered the Lord's Prayer Barbara and I were working ridiculously hard. But Love is Our Creators gift, so it is prayer, and not work, that we were needing. It was saying The Lord's Prayer that healed our lives and our relationship. It was The Father who is also Our Mother and the sacred rhythmic dance of their union, which enabled us to surrender to each other. The darkness gives way to light. The male embraces the female as she surrenders to receive him. Spirit fills us with life; like the energy created when cold and warm currents meet, as positive and negative ions unite, as male and female embrace and surrender to one another.

God is Our Father and Our Mother, Our Spouse, Our Brother, Our Sister, Our Child, Our Friend, even Our Enemy, and everyone is an opportunity to experience this dance called love.

The Lord's Prayer is designed to help us awaken to Christ as our pure and unconditionally receptive self. We are the children of Our Divine Father and Our Sacred Mother, and they are Our Deity: Love.

As we pray, we expand our giving and our receiving to realize why Christ, through Jesus, said, "You may only come to The Father through me". To receive the ultimate gift, we must become the ultimate vessel. Only Our Blessed Mother can receive Our Father. She is "The Christ" who was Jesus and the one who receives The Father within each of us.

SPIRITUAL EXERCISE: As we pray whether we are in male or female bodies it is our divine receptive feminine self who this prayer empowers. Use this prayer to embrace your Divine Feminine Self so you may actually receive, experience, and benefit directly from Our Fathers Holy Spirit. Ask Her to assist you in opening your heart and mind to let go and surrender to His love to receive. Become the feminine void surrendering, opening, and receiving. As you breathe in, feel your life and the whole universe flowing into you. As you breathe out feel the unconditionally loving light emanating from you.

NOTES:

_____
_____
_____
_____
_____

11. THE BEAST

When I was young my parents often told me how the key to a happy and successful life was getting a good education. Their enthusiasm was infectious and by the time I was five we were all extremely excited that I would soon be going to school. Then as I was getting out of my dad's car on that most important first day, he said, "Have a wonderful thirteen years' son". I quickly got back into his car. No one had said anything about thirteen years. I was just five. It sounded like a life sentence, but dad patiently explained about K-12. He assured me that I would be returning home from school every afternoon, so I finally went on to my first day of kindergarten.

First impressions often offer us a glimpse of our future. Prior to that first day I was a young boy primed and eager to learn but right from the beginning my kindergarten teacher and I seemed to be in conflict. First of all, she had no sense of humor, and she didn't seem to care what I wanted. To survive the boredom of her reality I learned to daydream with my eyes open. I also learned to be invisible and that my own self-esteem was more important than making her happy. With these lessons as the foundation of my education I went on to become unpopular with many teachers. Then one day I was a parent, and it was time for my own children to go to school.

I was determined that my kids would have better experiences than I had. I didn't have much faith in the

Public school system but was surprised to find that it was even worse than when I was a kid. I was feeling frustrated and powerless until my inner voice suggested I could give them a choice. For me school was always something I had to do and soon it was me against them (parents and teachers) and it was the feelings of abandonment that weighed heavy on my soul. Telling my kids that school was their choice was a little confusing at first but overall, I believe it gave them a healthier reality.

Tammy, our oldest, was the first to exercise her freedom of choice and one day her vice-principal called because she was "missing too much school". I told him it was her choice, and he was shocked and appalled. Then he threatened me and when that didn't work, he told me that "society is like a great machine and schools are for helping children become cogs and wheels within it". I had to laugh because he was right. The collective agreement of our male egos is indeed like a great machine, but when I told him that I hoped my children did not become cogs or wheels he hung up on me. After ignoring several threatening letters from the Los Angeles school board, Barbara and I were graciously invited to send our children to a wonderful "alternative public school". That school is proof that good public education is possible, and it is a testimony to the power and sanctity of free will. Our children thrived and began loving school.

As you can see Barbara and I are not typical parents and in part this is because as children we both took Peter Pans oath to never grow up to heart. As adults we both felt this oath honors the inner child as in Matthew 18:3: "become like little children." In 1989 Peter Pan was released again and that summer Barb and I took our children to see it. We were so excited that we would be sharing this magical experience with them. Looking forward to it was one of the highlights of our parenting experiences. But when the movie was over, we walked dismayed and deeply disappointed. Disney Inc. had removed the audience participation in taking Peter's oath. Why would they deprive our children of something so magical?

At first, we thought it must be a mistake, but another magical part of the movie was missing also. It was when Peter said that if we "believed", we could heal Tinkerbell by 'clapping our hands.' Sometime later we realized that the children who took Peters' oath in the 50's had become the "Flower Children" of the late 60's. And instead of "growing up" we protested the abusive male driven "Establishment". We rejected its heartless "Might Makes Right" policies and refused to become the cogs and wheels of its machinery. We believed in ourselves and love! It was a wonderful time until we began actively resisting. Jesus says, "Resist ye not evil" because resistance feeds the male ego and being creators, our resistance inevitably empowers what we resist.

The bible describes the machine of society as "The Beast" and it tells us that we have the authority to rule it. For a brief moment in the 60's many of us collectively agreed to honor peace and love over war and profits. In our innocence we became instruments of the Holy Spirit, and for just a moment our lives were magical until we broke our oath. Then we put our faith into artificial highs and ego trips, and it was over.

"The Beast" or establishment is constantly trying to control us because the one thing it fears is our child-like innocence. We're convinced that is why Disney removed the interactive audience participation in Peter Pans oath. And where Peter said, "If you believe, clap your hands" to heal Tinkerbell. It gave us faith in our ability to heal. As God's children, in our innocence, the Lord's Prayer is a powerful and affective spiritual weapon against the illusions of the world, "The Beast."

SPIRITUAL EXERCISE: Remember an experience when the Might Makes Right reality of The Beast threatened you. You may even be one who was threatening, it doesn't really matter. Observe what changes in you as you say the Lord's Prayer. Notice how your perception shifts. And how new possibilities present themselves as you simply pray and observe The Beast.

NOTES:

_____

_____

_____

_____

_____

_____

_____

_____

12. HOLOGRAPHIC UNIVERSE

To know peace or satisfaction in this world is challenging when nothing here is really as it seems. In 1991 Barb and I were given a remarkably interesting book called "The Holographic Universe". Its' author, Michael Talbot, weaves the ideas of cutting-edge scientists, psychologists, and theologians into a revolutionary new thesis. In this book Mr. Talbot introduces us to brilliant and courageous thinkers that collectively describe our universe as God's divine hologram.

The Holographic Universe translates complex scientific theories into a clear and simple, holographic model. In it Mr. Talbot explains why this theory is so unpopular with The Beast. The Wizards of Oz (huge egos) lose their edge when the veils of illusion they hide behind are lifted. And this is exactly what The Holographic Universe does. Holograms defy the linear cause and effect laws of physics ("for every action there is an equal and opposite reaction) which the Law of Moses (an eye for an eye) and our Western, sciences, religions and legal systems are all based on.

In his enlightening book Mr. Talbot describes how a hologram is created first by splitting a laser. Next a three-dimensional form is inserted into one of its' halves and both halves are reflected together to imprint a holographic film. Finally, a second laser is directed through the holographic film and a 360% projected image of the original form magically appears. We can walk around the hologram and from every angle it's a perfect replica of the original form.

In Genesis chapter I: the creation story begins as "God says Let there be light", and then "God created the heaven and the earth," and "God divided the light from the darkness," and "God divided the waters from the waters." God said, "let there be lights in the firmament of the heaven to divide the day from the night" and so forth. What Moses, the author of Genesis, is describing here is how creation begins with light and unfolds as the light divides in exactly the same way that a hologram is created!

Now comes the good part. If we break that holographic film into pieces and shine a laser through just one piece the whole original hologram appears. The quality is diminished but the whole form is present in every piece. For example: If the hologram is of a horse and we shine a laser through the piece of film containing the horse's ear the whole horse will appear. These phenomena explain how "The Kingdom of God is within us", why Jesus says that loving our neighbor is the same as loving God, and why he says, "I and my Father are one".

Realizing our universe is a hologram was one of the most exciting and enlightening experiences of my life. I'd always wondered why the spiritual teachers of the Far East said the whole universe was within each of us. In a Holographic Universe mysteries like ESP, premonitions and spiritual healing are easily understood. Even time travel, bi-location and material manifestation are possible for those, like Jesus, who learn to navigate this amazing holographic reality.

Not only are these "phenomena" possible they're even logical, but linear and holographic logic are not the same. There's a point in our understanding of the hologram where we must surrender to its' mysteries. We can observe what it does but how remains a mystery. Linear logic allows us to indulge our egos' desire for control, but its' linear illusions confine us to only the most superficial relationships. We can't control the universal hologram, but we can always trust its goodness. Our control-freak egos don't like trading their expectations for simple faith but that's the price for reality.

Since the dawn of history, we've been trying to control life. For thousands of years the linear, mental authority of our egos has ruled our hearts. Since Eden, the linear "Knowledge of Good and Evil" has supported the "Might Makes Right" philosophy empowering The Beast. Now Christ reveals the simple holographic wisdom of "Thy will be done". Listen carefully and you may hear Jesus, 2000 years ago, saying: "Our Creators universe is a hologram and I know you don't know what that is yet but in about 2000 years you will, and then this will all make a lot more sense".

SPIRITUAL EXERCISE: In this holographic universe everything is connected. This is why Jesus was able to heal and calm the storm and how our individual prayers profoundly affect the entire world. Think of someone you love or are concerned about. As you pray, see their spirits being healed and uplifted. Feel your two selves joined in faith, sharing the reality of the prayer and observe what happens. Do this for a full week and see how your relationship with them changes.

NOTES:

_____

_____

_____

_____

_____

_____

_____

_____

_____

_____

_____

_____

_____

_____

_____

_____

_____

_____

_____

_____

_____

_____

_____

_____

13. PLAYING GOD

Whatever happens in this life, no matter how wonderful
or terrible, the following is always true: It is always
God's will and always an opportunity for us to
learn and grow.

Over the past twenty years Barbara and I have received
many amazing blessings and some pretty painful and
frightening challenges. We've lost several businesses and
a house. At times we've evenhad to feed and shelter our
eight children on welfare. We've made plenty oftrips to
emergency rooms and had many sleepless nights praying
for our children and grandchildren. Along the way our
relationship has certainly been tested, and when no one
and nothing else could help us, The Lord's Prayer has
always provided exactly what we needed.

In 1990 Barbara and I manifested one of our dreams,
which was to own our own restaurant. "Barbara's Café"
was a wonderful place. Creating it and owning it was one
of the most wonderful and yet painful experiences of our
lives. With hindsight we now see that God had something
much better for us in store, but at the time we were just
trying to hold on to our dream. With everything we had
and all that we could borrow we resisted letting go, which
turned our dream into a real nightmare.

Back then Barb and I still believed that faith was about
God answering our prayers, yet the heart of this prayer is
not "<u>my will</u>", but "<u>Thy</u> will be done".

We were attached to our café and afraid of losing it until finally it was lovingly torn away from us. That was very painful and while we were fighting to keep our café our home went into foreclosure, so we fought even harder. When it was over our café and our house were both gone. We had a huge debt, no income, and no savings. We ended up on welfare and for a while, and we didn't even have a working car. Looking back, we can see that it wasn't being poor, but our fear of the unknown, that caused us to suffer at that time.

The irony is that our unknown future was full of blessings. By holding on to what we had with one hand and resisting the unknown with the other we were crucifying ourselves and postponing the blessings. Finally, losing everything opened the way for us to receive something much better. In fact, all along, God was preparing us to receive exactly what we'd been praying for. Having free will means we can play God to avoid change but playing God and resisting His/Her will is exhausting, and unfulfilling. Our willfulness blocks us from receiving the blessings His will is eager to provide.

Prior to having Barbara's' café, we both prayed often. But once we had our dream, we got busy maintaining it and stopped praying. With our dream came our fears that Gods' Will might be different than our own. Playing God is like driving a nice car without knowing where you want to go. There's an illusion of power, freedom, and possibilities but eventually you just run out of gas and finally let go.

During the time that Barbara's Café was open and while

our control-freak egos were desperately scavenging to keep us in business, we were also learning a lot about The Lord's Prayer. Contrast is a great teacher so holding on to our dream also taught us a lot about letting go.

The Lord's Prayer is like a road map or a blueprint. It helps us to focus our creative awareness to manifest a life better than we can imagine. It guides each of us to fulfil our soul's unique spiritual destiny. By honoring our souls' intent to receive Our Creators kingdom it carries us beyond the limits of our own desires, and this experience is what we call Surfing Love. Barbara and I believe that every one of us will eventually return to the heart of God. Life is a blessed circle, and we can't see Our Father breaking it with eternal damnation. Eternity is a long time, and we believe the time each of us spends playing God is how long it will take our souls to receive our ultimate blessing in the heavens.

SPIRITUAL EXERCISE: Think of something that you want or do not want, something you want to hold on to or something you hope to avoid. Feel your attachment and or resistance and say, "Lord this is what I want," or "This is what I do not want," and "Thy will be done". As you do this feel yourself relaxing and letting go. Do this a few times and say the Lord's Prayer. As you pray notice how each word is an opportunity to let go and let God. Repeat the prayer, relax, let-go and let-god.

Notes:_____

_____
_____
_____
_____
_____
_____
_____
_____
_____
_____
_____
_____
_____
_____
_____
_____
_____
_____
_____
_____
_____
_____
_____
_____
_____
_____
_____
_____

14. THE UNITY OF OPPOSITES

The unity of opposites is the dance of life, the fabric of our holographic universe, and the core of our human experience. We have left and right hands and feet, two eyes and two ears, but one mouth, because The Word is sacred. We also have a left and right brain with such different personalities that at times it seems we have two selves. Our conscious male, adult-mind, is very logical and rational but our subconscious, feminine, child-mind is emotional and intuitive. The relationship of these two opposite inner selves creates our individual realties in much the same manner that Our Creator manifests this universe through the interfacing forces of yin & yang or male and female.

Peace and joy are what we experience when the union between our two innerselves is cooperative and loving but our conflicts are also reflections of these inner relationships. Generally, our male-adult mind uses its worldly power and knowledge to intimidate and persuade the subconscious feminine-child. By placing a higher value on the male-adult we allow this abuse and deny ourselves joy, peace, and love. To have peace on earth we must love our neighbor, but first we must love ourselves; our whole self, both male and female aspects, and until we do our spirits will not rest.

The Beast (society) is the rational non-feeling product of our male adult mind. This mind is strongly associated with our ego, which says things like time is money, work hard to get ahead, and do whatever it takes. In school and at home we're rewarded for being mature, efficient adults and punished or penalized for being creatively playful, immature children. Gradually our feelings, from our inner child, shut down and our lives become dull, too logical, and not fun. That's when the Beast becomes our master. It rewards and controls us with money, titles, and false authority. But if we're unable to enjoy our lives what's the point?

We suppress our subconscious feeling mind because, like a child, it's difficult to control and because we don't understand how powerful it really is. However, it's through this inner child that the power of God's Holy Spirit flows into us. Like any abused child deep down it feels hurt, angry and alienated when suppressed. By surrendering to ride the Lord's Prayers' loving rhythms our inner child begins to heal. Jesus tells us to "Love God with our whole heart, mind and spirit" or our words will be vain as our faith is shallow. By "Receiving this little child in his name" we put heart and spirit into our prayers.

The Lord's Prayer also heals our inner child by speaking in two distinct languages. One is the adult language of words and the other, the child's language of symbols, feelings, and imagery. In this way the Lord's Prayer produces a peaceful holy ground where our two selves may mutually agree to embrace the unconditionally loving reality of Christ. I began to see these two languages one evening while contemplating some of the differences between the books of Matthew and Luke. In the heart of this prayer, Matthew says ("thy kingdom come, thy will be done, on earth as it is in heaven"). Luke says ("Thy Kingdom come, thy will be done, as it is in heaven so also in earth"). At first it seemed insignificant but then in Luke I saw the six pointed "Star of David". Jesus was a Jew, and this star is the symbol of the Hebrew faith.

In Luke, the heart of this prayer breathes with a rhythmic wave flowing from the inner reality of God's Kingdom, into our outer earthly lives. The heart rhythms of this prayer express its purpose. "Thy Kingdom is an **inner** reality, come is an **outer** reality, thy will (**inner**) be done (**outer**), as in heaven (**inner**) so also in earth" (**outer**). This star defines our purpose to be "The Light of this World" and also God's will to "Let there be Light". With this star in the prayer, it tells us it's all about opening our hearts which is what The Prayer Jesus Taught helps us do.

SPIRITUAL EXERCISE: The heart of this prayer is so rich it's a whole prayer in and of itself. Using three full breaths each time say**: Thy kingdom = (in breath), come (out breath); Thy will (in), be done (out): As it is in heaven (in), so also in earth (out).** As you breathe visualize and feel Gods loving light pouring into your heart and flowing out again. With every breath feel your heart opening and see your life flourishing. See everyone and everything being blessed by your prayers.

NOTES:_____

_____
_____
_____
_____
_____
_____
_____
_____
_____
_____
_____
_____
_____
_____
_____
_____
_____
_____

15. LET THERE BE LIGHT

Seeing the Star of David within the heart of the Lord's Prayer encouraged us to look deeper and soon another form was revealed. The Star of David is about birthing Our Father's light into our earthly lives and this second form shows how we embody The Light.

The Lord's Prayer is divided into three sections. First there are three attunements above the heart [chakras 1-3], 1. (Our Father), 2. (who art in heaven), 3. (hallowed be thy name). These three attunements are all about "The Father".

The heart attunement [chakra 4] in the form of a six-pointed star is about the "Holy Spirit", The Light, which is the unity of the Father and Son.

Below the heart are three more attunements [chakras 5-7]: 5. (Give us our daily bread), 6. (And forgive us). 7. (And lead us not into temptation). These lower three attunements are about "The Son". And the whole prayer clearly expresses the relationship called "The Holy Trinity."

Now this is where it gets magical. Connecting the upper and lower attunements of this prayer to the heart attunement we produce two tetrahedrons. What exactly is a tetrahedron? It's a three-sided pyramid and the simplest of all 3D forms. One point is a point. Two points is a line. Three points is a triangle, and these are all just flat 2D images (having two sides, or dimensions), but with four points we can create a tetrahedron having mass (3rd dimensional form).

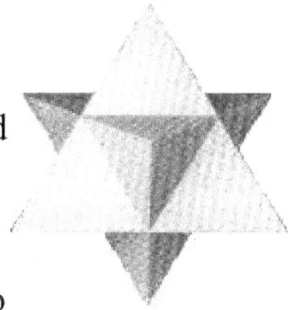

First the two tetrahedrons in the prayer define how the reality of The Father and The Son (ourselves) meet and become one as we open our hearts to the loving reality of Our Creator. As we do "Our eye is made single and our whole body is filled with light". This melding of our reality with God's in the prayer produces another exquisite geometric form. It's an eight-pointed "star-tetrahedron".

This star-tetrahedron is the foundational structure of every created thing so it's much like Our Fathers signature. This beautiful 3D star is found within the sacred sights of our most ancient and advanced civilizations where it was apparently known as the universal, geometric infrastructure of light. We will share a great deal more about this amazing form but for the moment let's just say that its presence in the prayer serves as a primordial trigger signaling and offering our sub-conscious mind an irresistible invitation for it to join us, wholeheartedly, in our prayers.

71

The star-tetrahedron is both a star and a cube. By simply connecting its' eight points like so (See fig.) we create a cube. Thus, the star (a symbol of light) within a cube (symbol of thephysical world) again defines our purpose to physically embody God's light ("As in heaven so also in earth").

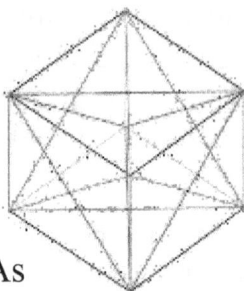

SPIRITUAL EXERCISE: As you say the prayer be aware of yourself as a bridge or doorway between the heavens and earth. Allow yourself to feel the heavenly realities of joy, peace and love pouring forth from you into the world around you. Be aware of every chakra as a radiant portal of God's Love. Experience yourself as "the light of the world". As you pray feel the loving inner reality of Gods light flowing out through you into the world. See the opposites in your life being healed and unified. See the reality of Love being born through you. Experience each attunement of this prayer as an affirmation of God's Kingdom being born through you into our world.

NOTES:

_____

_____

_____

_____

_____

_____

16. SPIRITUAL REALITY CHECK

To conclude Part II, we want to share what we call our "Spiritual Reality Check". Every attunement in the prayer presents us with an important question. Our answers to these questions, like the windows and our individual "Doors of Perception," profoundly affect how we experience our lives and ourselves. There are no right or wrong answers, but pure and simple answersprovide clear visions while complex and impure ones cloud our vision.

Your life is your own unique version of reality and what the Lord's Prayer enables us to do is trade in our limiting, inferior projections to receive God's perfect and unlimited awareness. It's the best deal in the universe but there are sacrifices involved. First, we must let go of our desire to be right. Then we must let go of our comfort zones. In the end we must be willing to accept that what our minds think we want is inferior to what our souls really need. Our perceptions are generally constructed from the information that we receive through our five senses but compared to the reality of our souls those are just one speck of sand on the beach.

One reason we value the Lord's Prayer so highly is because it enables us to change for the better very quickly. This spiritual reality check which the prayer contains helps us quickly focus on our most fundamental and important spiritual questions. The prayer illuminates where we are, where we want to be, and what we must do within ourselves to get there. This reality check is simple and self-evident. It's an excellent way of preparing to have a deeper experience of prayer and a deeper experience of life.

SPIRITUAL EXERCISE: Go through these questions slowly enough to feel your mental, emotional, and physical responses to them. There are no right or wrong answers. Don't think about these questions. Just let the answers rise up from your soul. The idea here is to reflect on our realities and to receive insights concerning that which we really need to pray.

SPIRITUAL REALITY CHECK EXCERCISE:

OUR: What does it mean to be God's child and God's family?

FATHER: Who is God? How do you see Him/Her?

WHO ART IN HEAVEN: What and where is your heaven?

HALLOWED BE THY NAME: What is God's name? What Makes it holy. How do you honor the sacredness of Your own thoughts?

THY KINGDOM COME: What is heavenly about your life?

THY WILL BE DONE: How does God's will affect and change you?

AS IT IS IN HEAVEN SO ALSO IN EARTH: What does heaven onearth look like to you? What are you doing there?

GIVE US THIS DAY OUR DAILY BREAD What do you want? Whatdo you need? How can you open more to receive it?

AND FORGIVE US AS WE FORGIVE What do you feel that you need to be forgiven for? What do you have to forgive them for?

AND LEAD US NOT INTO TEMPTATION: What tempts you?

DELIVER US FROM EVIL: What would you be delivered from?

FOR THYN IS THE KINGDOM AND THE POWER AND THE GLORY FOREVER: What is your ultimate dream?

AMEN: How committed are you to your own dream? How much areyou willing to give it? How much are you giving to it each day?

We find beginning our daily spiritual exercises with this "Spiritual Reality Check" enables us to move deeper and faster.

NOTES:

_____
_____
_____
_____
_____
_____
_____
_____
_____

PART III : SPIRITUAL WARRIORS

In Matthew 10:34 Jesus, the "Prince of Peace" says, "I do not bring peace to earth, but a sword". Why? We believe it's because we humans are a warrior race. Each of us, in our own way, is a fighter and a rebel. Our history is dominated by wars. For 2000 years we've fought over "the truth" but in all that time we've been missing the real point. Jesus, our personal hero, is the ultimate rebel because the point of the ultimate sword is love. Love, the power of Christ within us, is our egos master and why "The Beast" had Jesus killed.

On CNN, I heard a tape made by Osama Bin Ladin. He was saying how the world will now be split and that a final "holy war" will take place between "the believers and non-believers". At first, I felt sad that a soul could mistake hate for faith, but then I was surprised to find myself agreeing with him. I too see the world as being divided between believers and non-believers. And I do believe it is time for a holy war. But the non-believers who blame, create fear, hate and fight for control are not the holy warriors. Those who fight the enemy within us, with love and compassion, as Jesus did, are the "believers" and true "spiritual warriors".

The old law of an eye for an eye fueled by ego has gradually, over time, escalated war to this crucial point when we who are the true warriors of the universe must fight in this new way. Jesus brings God's holographic law of 'Love'. This law is our swords point and the one with which Christ, through us, conquers The Beast. A spiritual warrior does not attack or defend. She courageously opens his/her heart to receive and to express God's will / which is 'Love'.

I believe those of us living here at this time have signed on to create the peace we've dreamed of from our souls beginning. It may sound impossible, but it could not be more perfect. God is Love so the needs of our human family represent the greatest spiritual opportunity imaginable.

As we say, "Lord this is my prayer for peace in my own life, and Thy Will be done," are opening our hearts to become the instruments of Love. This is how we become the "sword" of Christ and true "spiritual warriors". And this is what the Lord's Prayer also helps us to do.

Inwardly take a moment now and say:

"Our Father, Who Art in Heaven. Hallowed by Thy Name. Thy kingdom come, thy will be done, as it is in heaven so also in earth. Give us this day our daily bread and forgive us our trespasses as we forgive those who trespass against us. And lead us not into temptation but deliver us from illusion. (evil)

17. DESIRE

Barbara and I are two vastly different people. What we desire from our lives and from each other is vastly different. Our differences have presented many challenges and difficulties, but when we surrender to God's will they become opportunities. Our differences create space between us, but we need not be separated by this space. When we're attached to our own desires our egos fill that space with struggles and conflicts. When we let-go God fills that same space with love and our relationship becomes much more than the sum of our two individual selves.

Nothing we know of can help us to let go the way the Lord's Prayer does. As we've shown you, its design is very harmonious with our own, and that's one reason it is so effective. The structure of our consciousness is like a pyramid. It has four sides, a capstone, eight levels and a base. It even has mystical passages leading to sacred inner chambers. Here and now, we're going to focus on just the base of this pyramid which is desire.

Desire defines our lives, enables us to grow and to evolve. Desire is why we fight, work, compete, eat, and make love. We are conceived through desire. Our thoughts and even our breath come from desire. So do our habits, our inspirations, our creativity, and our suffering. We feel hurt and or angry when our desires are blocked and happy when they are fulfilled. Desire melds our physical, mental, and emotional bodies into one passionate, creative force. And to suppress a desire is to deny a God given creative opportunity.

Desire is what our base chakra and its attunement, "Lead us not into temptation but deliver us from evil", is about. To be "delivered" from "evil" (illusion) we must surrender. To be free from temptation, to receive Our Fathers blessings we must ask for what we want but then be willing to let our desires go! This or something better for the highest good. And this is what the ancient sacrificial rituals were about. But for a sacrifice to be fruitful our hearts and intentions must be pure, and this is why we pray.

As you know Barb and I have a large family and that's probably why, to us, desires seem to be a lot like children. We need to love and honor them but it's also important that we don't indulge them. Like children our desires feed on our attention, they inspire our hopes, but they also disappoint us. It's not their fault because, like children, our desires reflect exactly what we give to them.

In the end, to be happy, we must own what we want but trust that by then giving it all to God will manifest more than our humanly desires could ever imagine!

God's love is the ultimate desire of every soul but lessor desires, "false gods", prevent us from realizing this until we say, "Lord this is what I want, and Thy will be done". Otherwise, our lesser desires will continue to grow and become our addictions, obsessions, and burdens. The bigger they grow the harder we must try either to control and or to satisfy them until eventually we collapse and have to let go. That's the hard way because by just saying "Thy will be done" the same and much more is accomplished.

All desires are potent reservoirs of life force, and the Lord's Prayer enables us to put their powerful energies to work for us. As we let them go in our prayers those energies that have held us back are released. By letting go in this way those lesser desires that have held us down actually propel our spirits upward. Now our biggest challenges become our greatest opportunities. As we say "Lord this is what I want, and Thy will be done" we resolve our internal conflicts. By focusing only on our truest and highest desire we become peacemakers and spiritual warriors. Now our age-old human drama of fighting for what we want ends, and our dream of peace on earth begins.

SPIRITUAL EXERCISE: To get in touch with this primal condition called desire we suggest that you let all the air out of your lungs. Now hold it out as long as you can without straining. Observe how your desire to take a breath grows and grows until you finally let go and breathe. Now do this again and be aware of how this desire to breathe is also your desire to live. Now do it again and observe what you believe will help you to live your life more fully. Observe what you believe will make your life more loving. Own these desires. They are your opportunity to say, "Lord this is what I want, and Thy Will be done". Now as you say the Lord's Prayer you may feel a greater freedom to give and a greater openness to receive. All that limits us are the desires we possess as they possess us until we let go and let God.

NOTES:

_____
_____
_____
_____
_____
_____
_____
_____
_____
_____
_____
_____
_____
_____
_____
_____
_____
_____

18. CRUCIFIXION

Wanting, attaching, resisting and willful fighting stretches and stresses us until we reach our breaking point. This experience is called crucifixion and then we finally let go. It's how and where we come to realize that there's really nothing we can do but let go. Crucifixion is painful and humiliating as long as we're holding on, and avoidance just prolongs our suffering. In the end we all must let go. The question is how long do we need to suffer? In the Lord's Prayer we choose to embrace crucifixion to help us enjoy the heavenly gifts here in our earthly lives.

In my previous life as an inventor, I thought I wanted to succeed more than anything. When I actually sold my first invention (the game) to Sears the taste of success was so sweet. Two years later and just days before we were to send out our first shipment, the liability insurance on my game jumped from $50,000 a year to $500,000. Six months after that when we were finally ready to ship again Sears had a crisis. It was the only year in Sears' history when they did not show a profit, and all new product lines were frozen for two years. The buyer, who gave us the order, was transferred to another department and finally our manufacturer backed out of the deal. Ugh!

I pulled out of that disappointment and went on to invent an exercise device called "The Total Trainer". After a couple more years of hard work and a large investment of my time and money, I once again had an order for my new product. And once again, days before we were ready to ship, we had a fundamental problem. It was inconvenient but not the end of the world, not until my three partners all freaked and started suing each other and me. I didn't have the money to fight them, so I resigned as the president of Progressive Fitness Inc., signed over my stock in the company and all my rights to our patents. I had to let go.

At first, I did let go but I didn't let God, and I didn't have the strength to rebound. I sank into a deep depression and when I realized that God wasn't going to let me succeed that way, I sank even deeper. It didn't seem fair but, not knowing what else I could do, I started to pray. Feeling totally humbled and very vulnerable I said, "Lord I really do want this. I want to make lots of money to take care of my family and to have a really good life; and Thy will be done". That's when I saw my seven-year-old self and when my life suddenly got easier, happier, and more magical. After that experience I felt like a child again. My new life was like a dream and writing this book is an important part of that dream.

Jesus could say "my burden is light, and my yoke is easy" because he was an expert at releasing his worldly desires as spiritual ballast. They say he suffered for our sins, but I believe Jesus loved his life and suffered because he too struggled with not wanting to let it go. It's ironic that spiritual awareness and freedom make our human lives much more pleasurable and passionate. Passion fuels our desires, our attachments, and our resistance to loss. This dilemma is graphically portrayed in the crucifixion. The cost of caring deeply and livingfully is the pain of letting go. The cost of not caring and not living is having nothing to let go of and nothing to propel our spirits into the heavens.

EXERCISE: Within each attunement there is a cross defining our experience of crucifixion on that level (see below). Observe and feel the stress connected to each cross (+). Use the questions to reflect on how each cross is also an opportunity to let go ("Thy will be done"). Begin at the base, #1. (Wanting) and work your way up to #8 (Aware). Affirm each cross, "I am wanting", and then say, "Thy will be done". Feel yourself releasing all the stress you have connected with each cross while breathing and releasing in each chakra. When you feel complete say the prayer and let go even more.

NOTES:

_____
_____
_____
_____
_____
_____
_____
_____
_____
_____
_____

EIGHT CROSSES (+)

8. ALL CHOKRAS: *FOR THYN* (+AWARE)
I am Aware. What are you happy to be aware of? What don't you want to be aware of?

7. CROWN: *OUR FATHER* (+ACCOMPLISHING)
I am Accomplishing. What do you want to accomplish? How do you resist accomplishing?

6. THIRD EYE: *IN HEAVEN* (+SEEKING or SEEING)
I am Seeing. Who or what are you looking for? What don't you want to see?

5. THROAT: *THY NAME* (+COMMUNICATING)
I am Communing. What do you want to say? What don't you want to hear?

4. HEART: *THY WILL* (+CARING)
I am Caring. What do you care about? How is caring a problem for you?

3. SOLOR PLEXUS: *DAILY BREAD* (+RESPONDING)
I am Responding. How do you want to respond? How do you want to be responded to?

2. NAVEL: *FORGIVE US* (+KNOWING)
I am Knowing. What do you want to know? What don't you want to know?

SEXUAL: *TEMPTATION* (+WANTING)
I am Wanting. What do you want? What don't you want?

NOTES:

_____

_____

_____

_____

19. CROSSES & PEARLS

It's true that our finest human accomplishments come from our greatest challenges, and we believe that's why Jesus said, "To ascend you must pick up your cross and follow me". From the beginning working with the Lord's Prayer has confronted me with my own greatest challenge. It's my lifelong desire to prove my self-worth to my family, teachers, and critics. How could I ever hope to achieve "success" by devoting my life to this prayer?

Seven years after committing ourselves to this prayer Barbara and I had been richly blessed. We were finally successful and then were asked by spirit to do something pretty crazy. We were instructed to sell our new home in Venice Beach, to abandon our thriving new business and move our big family to Durango Colorado. (Population 12,000). We didn't know why we were being guided there or what we would do there. Naturally everyone, ourselves included, thought we'd lost our minds, yet the ease of our move and the great price we got for our house helped to reassure us that we were doing the right thing.

Soon after arriving in Durango Barbara and I started receiving tremendous praise and support for our work sharing what we had learned from The Lord's Prayer. That's when we began to understand how this move was an answer to our prayers. We had been praying for this opportunity a long time but to my surprise I was totally unprepared to receive it. I'd grown up playing the role of the rebel. I could take criticism and even punishment, but praise and respect made me quite uneasy. Until we moved to Durango "The way of cross" was a concept I thought I understood but understanding it and living it are worlds apart.

Seeing our work changing people's lives and receiving sincere gratitude and praise was rewarding. But for reasons I didn't understand this also made me feel extremely vulnerable. Soon every Monday night our living room was full of people who came to hear me talk and to pray with us. Our home was becoming a church, which is exactly what we'd prayed for. We were also booked solid with private counseling appointments and people back in LA were setting up workshops for me. Everything we'd hoped for, and much more was happening. Feeling the Holy Spirit using us to bless others was awesome, but the better things got the more vulnerable I felt.

Finally, just before a big workshop in LA I nearly had a heart attack and I had to stop teaching for two years. During those years I learned to embrace my fears as allies and I realized how "Thy Kingdom come, Thy will be done" is the key to the hidden secrets of this prayer. Jesus says, "the Kingdom of God is like unto a merchant man, seeking goodly pearls: Who, when he had found one pearl of great price, went and sold all that he had, and bought it". The obvious message here is that God's kingdom is the ultimate treasure but there's also a deeper one about creativity.

A pearl begins with a grain of sand, which, to the oyster, is a life-threatening irritant. The oyster embraces the sand and after time the result is a beautiful and valuable pearl, a spherical symbol of unity and purity. Like the oysters' grain of sand our own cross helps us to manifest our most precious gifts. Every cross is a pearl waiting to be born. But to transform a weakness into strength, or suffering into beauty, or fear into genius requires the courage of a spiritual warrior.

Now in this next spiritual exercise we will embrace the eight crosses from the last chapter as grains of sand. From each cross we will create a pearl and every pearl represents a different dimension of letting go. Each cross and every pearl is a powerful human feeling. As you explore your feeling relationships to them, they will open your feeling heart to the Lord's Prayer in new ways. The result will be much more powerful and effective prayers.

See next page:

✝ = Crosses: ξ = Pearls:

8. *FOR THYN IS THE KINGDOM*
✝AWARE - ξ LOVING.

7. *OUR FATHER*
✝ACCOMPLISHING - ξ FREEDOM.

6. *IN HEAVEN*
✝SEEKING ξ – PEACEFUL.

5. *HALLOWED BE THY NAME*
✝COMMUNING ξ – JOYFUL.

4. *THY KINGDOM COME*
✝CARING ξ – GRATEFUL.

3. *DAILY BREAD*
✝RESPONDING ξ –APPRECIATING.

2. *FORGIVE US AS WE FORGIVE*
✝KNOWING ξ – ACCEPTING.

1. *TEMPTATION*
✝WANTING ξ – LETTING-GO

EXERCISE: This exercise is similar to the last one. Breathe into the base chakra and affirm **"I am wanting" (in breath) and "I am letting-go" (out breath).** On the in breath feel the tension of wanting. On the out breath feel the surrender of letting go. Now move to the next chakra and affirm **"I am knowing"** (in) and **"I am accepting"** (out) then move on to the next level. After **"I am loving"** on the eighth level say the prayer and let go fully.

20. ORIGINAL SIN / ORIGINAL FEAR

Have you ever felt like something was wrong or about to go wrong, but you didn't know what? Have you ever felt naked or exposed but you weren't really sure why? Have you ever felt afraid for no apparent reason? Of course, you have, you're alive and such irrational fears are just part of our human experience. Like Jesus, The Holy Spirit is constantly telling us that there is more to our lives than we know but we're afraid of the unknown. This is why we avoid the greater heavenly reality just beyond the reach of our five senses. But what are we really afraid of?

Jesus feared the unknown. In the final days of his life, he even asked if God would do a last-minute rewrite. He said, "Lord I don't want to play this final scene; and Thy will be done". Then nearly his last words were "Father, Father why have you forsaken me". Did God abandon Jesus? Of course not! Jesus was exposing our ultimate irrational human fear. The one that cripples and prevents every one of us from being all that we can be until we find the courage, as spiritual warriors, to let go and trust that we are always being loved.

When I was a child, in catechism, the nuns told us that we'd inherited the sin of Adam and Eve and that unless this "Original Sin" was washed from our souls in baptism, we would go to this really boring place called Purgatory. As a child I didn't have a clue what they were talking about and before I could figure it out, I became an agnostic. Then several years ago, to my surprise, "Original Sin" started making sense to me, but differently than it had been conveyed to me in my youth. In the Garden of Eden Eve eats the "bad" apple after the serpent tells her "In the day ye eat thereof, your eyes shall be opened, and ye shall be as gods, knowing good and evil". Then Eve gave the fruit to Adam, he ate it, and "the eyes of both of them were opened, and they knew that they were naked". Next "they sewed fig leaves together, and made themselves aprons" and God asked, "why are you hiding and covering yourselves". Adam said, "I heard thy voice, and I was afraid, because I was naked, and I hid myself". God then asks, "Who told you that you were naked"?

Finally, just before Adam and Eve leave paradise God said, "Behold Adam has become as one of us knowing good and evil" and now they must "Leave and live by the sweat of their brows". In other words, "Now that they are creators, exercising their free will, they must learn to create a paradise of their own". But over the thousands of years since Eden we seem to have wandered further and further from paradise. Why? It comes back to our Original Sin/Fear. All we've really been doing down here is creating more and more elaborate fig leaves (defenses) but responding to fear is not the way to paradise: Responding to God's love is.

The Church tells us that baptism cleanses our soul. In Matthew 3:11 John the Baptist says, "I indeed baptize you with water, but he that cometh after me shall baptize you with the Holy Ghost and with fire". This baptism is our submersion in The Holy Spirit, which begins as we say "Lord, Thy Will be done" but then we must let go and with every breath we have an opportunity to let go more.

On the cross Jesus was obviously still struggling with his own faith when he asked "Father, Father why have you forsaken me"? But then in his final gasp he said, **"It is done."** Like Jesus as long as we live and breathe, we will be letting go. As we say, "Thy will be done we begin submerging ourselves in His Holy Spirit and with each breath we go deeper until in our last breath, our last letting go, we too will know; "it is done."

SPIRITUAL EXERCISE: As you say the prayer imagine that you're perfect just the way you are. Allow the prayer to help you release all those ideas and beliefs that make you feel defensive, afraid, or insecure. Breathe, let go and be conscious of God's perfection in your life. As you pray feel yourself surrendering, stripping, and becoming naked. Feel your naked heart and naked mind receiving Gods Love in new ways. Be vulnerable and awaken to the reality of Our Fathers Unconditional Love and protection. With every breath surrender to receive more and more and more. "For everything under heaven there is a season". Let this be the season to be greedy for His Love.

NOTES:

_____
_____
_____
_____
_____
_____

21. THE GAME of LIFE

Barbara and I find it's helpful to view our lives as a magnificent God-given game. Our Father contributes the game board, the raw materials, the rules, and our reward for winning is greater and greater acceptance of His Love. But how each of us play our game is up to each individual. What we choose and how we play defines the unique qualities of our individual lives. Realizing how Our Father supports us in every choice can make our games both fun and interesting but this freedom comes with a price. To play our games masterfully we must create responsibly, as Jesus did, and to do this we must search our own soul in prayer.

Wise men tell us that objectivity enables us to live and to create more effectively and efficiently. They are right but with the "Pearl of Great Price" (unconditional love) comes an extreme way of living and creating that defies all our earthly lessons. It's no secret that our assumptions and expectations make disappointed fools of us. But there is such a thing as divine expectation. It's the expectation that we are always and everywhere perfectly loved and the more willing we are to accept this, the more magical and rewarding our game of life becomes.

We all want to win, and we all want to be happy, but no one can tell us how. Winning is different for each of us because our adversaries, our egos, are so unique. Our rules of right and wrong, our ideas concerning winners, losers, heroes, villains, good and evil, failure and success are all very different.

What we have in common is that all our egos rules for winning are endlessly complex, extremely restrictive and in the end, they lead us nowhere. Both your ego and mine insist that the name of the game is CONTROL, but its real name is SURRENDER. And the Lord's Prayer is the instruction template; Jesus' masterful plan for winning the game of life through surrender.

That first night when I saw my seven-year-old self, believing so deeply in the Lord's Prayer, I could feel how much I missed his pure, innocent hopes and dreams. When I embraced him though, my ego laughed and taunted me the way the Roman soldiers had done to Jesus. My ego said I was desperate and naive, and he was absolutely right. It was desperation that originally caused me to abandon my inner child so of course it was desperation that reunited us again. Desperation leads to losing until we realize there's really nothing to lose. Then with a touch of faith, a little luck, and a bit of irony our egos' vast labyrinth of illusions wear us down. When we stop and simply let go, our egos battle cry ("My will be done") is replaced with Christs' promise ("Thy kingdom come, Thy will be done").

I don't know when I started following my ego, but it was probably when I realized that God wasn't fulfilling my expectations. My expectation that He was *supposed* to do my will, lead to many great disappointments. My inner child expects miracles, but it does not play God. It does not define what should happen, nor how, and yet it always knows that something wonderful and miraculous is happening.

I've received permission to embrace this child inner through simple logic: **"If God is the all-powerful and all loving Creator of this universe; If He/She is our ever-present Father and Mother then everything without exception, no matter how bleak or painful, must be to bless us"**.

Though this makes perfect sense, for most of us, the cooperating, illusionary indoctrinations of our five senses, our cynical egos and 'The Beast' (society) makes accepting this simple truth incredibly challenging. That's ok, God doesn't expect us to have blind faith! Approach your game of life as an experiment with the premise that "absolutely everything that happens in your life is to bless you." And remember you don't have to understand how you are being blessed to know that you are. Live your life in the assumption that you are unconditionally loved, and you will begin creating your own special heaven on earth; and that's how we win this game of life.

SPIRITUAL EXERCISE: Remember a time when you were hurt or disappointed. Look at what you wanted to happen and especially what you wanted to experience. Now let it go. Say Lord "this is what I wanted, but Thy will be done". Now pray in the assumption that you are perfectly loved and cared for in every way. Open your mind to see everything as a blessing. Don't expect anything good to happen but trust that everything good is already happening. Know that you are being blessed and loved right now. Feel Gods' Love gently lifting you just as fast as you are willing and able to let go. As you pray be aware that every attunement of this prayer is an opportunity to be loved.

NOTES:

22. SURFING THE FLAME

While our egos strive to bend reality, our inner child wants to honor Our Fathers' will, and we must choose. Do we fight for control or surrender to His love? Our egos make us feel that fighting to control is much safer and easier but being Gods' child is not about taking it easy or playing it safe. Deep down each of us wants to be the best person we can be and that's who the Lord's Prayer helps us to become. The bible describes our highest earthly transformation as "The baptism of the Holy Spirit with fire" and this experience of "The Rapture" is what the Lord's Prayer prepares us for.

The "Holy Spirit" is described in the bible as "tongues of fire". Our Father is called "The All-Consuming Flame" and "The Father of Lights". He is depicted, in Moses' vision, as a "Burning Bush" and Our Creators first words are "Let there be light". His heavens are adorned with flaming stars and Jesus tells us that we, His children, are "The lights of this world". The very foundation of creation is waves of pure light so it's not surprising to us that the Lord's Prayer also contains a constellation of eight brilliant stars.

These eight radiant expressions of our higher, "en**light**ened" selves are one of the most powerful useful tools that Barbara and I have received from the Lord's Prayer. They were revealed to us through the eight "pearls" (Chapter 19). Since then, we have constantly been amazed at how profoundly and quickly they have shifted our consciousness, awakening a full spectrum of 'Loving,' in us enhancing every aspect of our lives.

While the attunements in the Lord's Prayer bring heavenly light into our earthly bodies, these eight stars release the heavenly light trapped within our earthly bodies. Once you are familiar with them you will feel how they literally ignite your chakras. You may observe how the prayer and these stars complement each other and how using them together moves your spiritual awareness on a fast track towards "enlightenment".

These eight stars are present both within us and in the Lord's Prayer. By simply affirming them, like so: (1. I am letting-go, 2. I am accepting, 3. I am appreciating, 4. I am grateful, 5. I am joyful, 6. I am peaceful, 7. I am free and 8. I am loving"), we affirm our higher, radiant spiritual nature. As we attune to the radiance of each star, from "I am letting-go" to "I am loving"; we move our spiritual awareness higher and higher.

By affirming these eight luminous aspects within us, our worldly attachments and desires for control gently dissolve into light. So do our fears, confusion, doubts, and our suffering.

LETTING-GO enables us to **ACCEPT**.
ACCEPTING enables us **APPRECIATE** and to be **GRATEFUL**. From **GRATITUDE** comes **JOY**.
JOY lifts us into **PEACE**. In
PEACE we are **FREE** to be ourselves and
FREE to give and to receive what we want most, **LOVE**.
And **LOVE** transforms our lives magically and quickly for the better.

The EIGHT FLAME ATTUNEMENTS

8. Our Father = (I AM LOVING)
7. Our Father = (I AM FREE)
6. Who Art In Heaven = (I AM PEACEFUL)
5. Hallowed Be Thy Name = (I AM JOYFUL)
4. Thy Kingdom Come = (I AM GRATEFUL)
3. Give Us This Day = (I AM APPRECIATING)
2. Forgive Us As We Forgive = (I AM ACCEPTING)
1. Deliver us from evil [the outer illusions]= (I AM LETTING GO)

SPIRITUAL EXERCISE, (SURFING THE FLAME): Affirm and feel the radiance of each star in your body, mind, and emotions. Imagine a candleflame or better yet light a candle and observe how each star is present both in the flame and within you. Observe how the flame is **LETTING-GO** of itslight, effortlessly **ACCEPTING** fuel and oxygen. See how it radiates **APPRECIATION, GRATITUDE** and **JOY**. Observe how it is at **PEACE, FREE** to simply be and to LOVE. In **LOVE** the flame completes the circle of life, as we all do, by simply **LETTING-GO**. Now as you pray experiencethe radiant light that each attunement affirms and releases within you. We call this experience of surrendering to our own flame essence, Surfing the Flame.

23. RESURRECTION

Immortality is perhaps our ultimate mortal fantasy, probably because it's thetrue condition of our souls. When I was four, around the same time that I saw the movie Peter Pan with my grandmother, I remember asking my mother how long we would live. She said, if we were very lucky, we could live to be one hundred. Kids that age often still identify with their immortal souls, and that was the case with me because at first, I was sure she was mistaken and then I remember feeling extremely disappointed and sad that our earthly lives would be so short.

One of Barbara's favorite scriptures is, *"I am the resurrection and the life. Whosoever liveth and believeth in me shall never die".* Christ speaking through Jesus is telling us that our ultimate fantasy is in fact possible. By surrendering to the Christ within us, as Jesus did, we may resurrect ourselves from this moral illusion. And that's the bottom line of the prayer that Jesus taught: "For Thyn is the Kingdom and the power and the glory **forever.** Amen."

Jesus says, *"The first of all commandments is….Love the Lord thy God with all thy heart, and with all thy mind, and with all thy strength,"….And the second is like the first; Thou shalt love thy neighbor as thy self. There is no other commandment greater than these."*

But how do we love God, or our neighbor, when we are feeling unworthy and unlovable ourselves? And for that matter what does Our Heavenly Father really need from us? Being a father myself I know the greatest gift my children can give to me is just their willingness to receive my love.

By just saying "THANK YOU LORD" we open our hearts to receive Our Fathers love. Saying, "I LOVE YOU LORD" deepens our sense of appreciation and opens our hearts to Him even more. By saying "Thank you, I LOVE YOU Father" we also confront our fears of unworthiness. Does God need our love? I don't know. It seems unlikely but our highest God-given instinct is to love, and by expressing our love to Him we affirm our true value as we open our hearts to receive His grace.

The way I understand grace has a lot to do with my own sense of worthiness or rather unworthiness. I experience grace when I am receiving more than I feel I deserve. And since there is no way that any of us can really earn Our Fathers Love, His grace is ever-present. If we could earn God's love, then we could control our experience of Him. Then we would not experience vulnerability, nor would we ever have to surrender. My ego likes the sound of that but if I could earn Gods love then my life would never be magical, there would be no miracles, no grace and no such thing as unconditional love.

Our fears of unworthiness separate us from Our Father, but they also enable us to receive His grace. When Jesus says, "I in and of myself can do nothing" he's telling us that he is totally dependent on God and that's how we all enter into His grace. But then Jesus boldly says; "I am the way, the truth and the life" so how do these two quite different realities exist in one Jesus? They can and do because Jesus is a multi-dimensional being, as we all are. Jesus the man learned the way to eternity. Jesus the Christ embodied the truth of eternity and the Christ who was Jesus said, "I am the resurrection and the life. Whosoever liveth and believeth in me shall never die."

Worthy or not, Christ, The Holy Spirit, and Our Father all live within us. By saying "THANK YOU LORD, I LOVE YOU", without a reason, we move beyond our ego's reasonable boundaries into the reality of God and a whole new genesis begins. The Old Genesis was the story of God birthing us. Our Father says I am the Alpha and Omega. He is the beginning; we are His last creation, and this "New Genesis" is the story of us birthing Him. As we say, "THANK YOU & I LOVE YOU LORD", we embrace the circle of life. By giving and receiving in the same breath with the same words we dissolve the self-created, internal, boundaries that separate us from Our Divine Source.

Saying, "Thank you and I love you" we surrender the "hardness of our hearts" so our mortal selves may ascend, in resurrection, to eternal life.

SPIRITUAL EXERCISE: We cannot over emphasize the power of this exercise when taken to heart. As you breathe in say THANK YOU and feel gratitude for this breath of life. As you breathe out say I LOVE YOU to the inner source of your life/breath. On each in-breath receive the gift of life and say THANK YOU. On each out breath express your love to The Source of your life by saying I LOVE YOU LORD.

As you breathe, feel love flowing into you and be grateful. As you breathe out say I LOVE YOU and feel it flowing back again to God. As you say THANK YOU & I LOVE YOU LORD claim your freedom to always and everywhere be in love. With each breath feel your life force growing as God returns and multiplies your love. Take this exercise into each challenge and every relationship and your world will be magically transformed more quickly than you can imagine.

NOTES:

_____
_____
_____
_____
_____
_____
_____
_____
_____
_____
_____
_____
_____
_____
_____
_____
_____
_____
_____
_____

24. MELCHIZEDEK

In 1988 I was inwardly guided to create an incredibly distinctive design (See fig.). Right away Barbara and I started seeing symbols, patterns, and messages, in it, which helped us greatly in our work with the Lord's Prayer. We explored this fascinating design in some detail but here we are going to focus on just a few of its messages.

Our first message from this design came before it was even complete. Using a mixing bowl and 474 quarters I began by placing the quarters around the bowl until there were seven complete rings. Then I noticed how these rings seemed to be pulsing and it felt like they were actually trying to communicate something to me. Next, I was guided to count the quarters in these seven rings and there were 294 of them. Then Barbara remembered a book we had on the Qabalah, the mystical spiritual science of the Hebrews. Looking in this book I discovered that in this ancient science the number 294 (7x42) is the number representing Melchizedek.

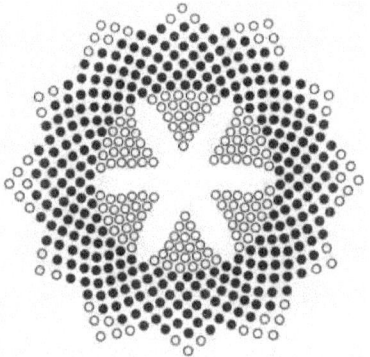

I went to the bible where I read how this powerful and mysterious man was known as the "King of Salem". In Gen. 14: 18 he's described as "the priest of the most High

104

God". In Hebrews 5: 6, the bible says "Thou (Jesus) art a priest forever after the order of Melchizedek. Finally in Hebrews 7: 3 we find this concerning Melchizedek. "He is the king of peace; Without father, without mother, without decent, having neither beginning of days, nor end of life; but made like unto the Son of God; abideth a priest continually."

Now consider how great this man was unto whom even the patriarch Abraham gave a tenth of the spoils". From the beginning of our journey with The Lord's Prayer Barbara and I felt we were being directed by a benevolent intelligence, but we didn't know who or what was guiding us. Now for the first time, as we were discovering who Melchizedek was, we felt very connected to him. But here we're going to share just a couple of important messages from this amazing design.

When the whole design was complete, we saw it's 474 dots as being symbolic of our human souls. Each is a perfect, whole circle participating in a much larger radiant design. God's will ("Let there be light") is present here and like our sun it is a twelve-pointed star with six major and six minor rays. In the Qabalah 474 is the number for unity, and this is what the Lord's Prayer is about. In its center we see a flower, symbolic of our souls as the blooms of 'Our Fathers' creation. Bit by bit this fascinating design has given us insights both into ourselves and into the depth of the Lord's Prayer but there's one special insight that we find is especially helpful in our prayers.

Only after many hours of contemplation did we see a

perfect spider in the design. Neither of us were too fond of spiders we were living in Southwestern Colorado at the time and surrounded by Native Americans whose view of the spider helped us to see something very beautiful and important in it. To the Ute, Navaho, Hopi, and the Zuni, Spider is the creator who weaves the patterns and designs of life. Once we got beyond our creepy, crawly prejudices we saw how Spider was offering us a crucial insight into the process that we call prayer.

First of all, Spiders structural form clearly reflects the same core creative patterns that are in the Lord's Prayer. Example: Spiders two antenna express the duality of our minds, and her eight legs, four on either side, wonderfully portrays how the eight-pointed star-tetrahedron is constructed. Her hourglass shape even seems to mimic our symbol for infinity or eternity but the insight we wish to explore here is about how Spider creates by using her web quite masterfully.

Our human thoughts are often described as webs and the human race is notorious for "getting tangled up in its own webs". Spider has helped us to see the Lord's Prayer as a divine instruction for manifesting the ultimate thought, or web. Spider creates by using her web to attract and receive her worldly needs, and we now see the Lord's

Prayer as having a similar purpose.

As we pray, we carefully weave our web (our prayer). Then we must patiently wait. We do not look for what we want. We wait and listen for the subtle blessings present in every breath. Our prayers gently expand our perception and our ability to receive our simplest and smallest blessings. Until we can do this how can we ever hope to receive our greater ones? The more we focus, the more deeply we care and the more sincerely we feel our prayers, and the stronger and better our web becomes. The more patiently we wait, listening and feeling, and the more we open to receive God's blessings the more we may receive them. Jesus taught this prayer to help us realize the heavenly blessings within our earthly lives. As we do our faith in Our Fathers love for us grows and this realization is our gateway to the heavens.

SPIRITUAL EXERCISE: As you pray pay close attention; pray sincerely, listen deeply, feel fully, and let go to accept God's love in every moment with every breath. Know that if you do not experience yourself receiving or being loved it's just because you need to let go more. Be aware of the magnetic quality of your prayer or web, and your expectations of positive results will be fulfilled. As you pray allow these expectations to grow and release them the way Spider releases her silky threads.

As you wait and listen, between your prayers, imagine the web you're creating extending throughout and beyond your awareness. Know that wherever and whenever your web receives a blessing you can feel it so keep creating, waiting, and knowing that you are always and everywhere being loved and blessed beyond your imagination. Extend the consciousness of your heart and mind beyond the current boundaries of your thoughts. Remember the goal is not to attract Our Fathers Love but to feel, and to receive it by letting go of everything else.

NOTES:_____

_____
_____
_____
_____
_____
_____
_____
_____
_____
_____
_____
_____
_____
_____
_____
_____
_____
_____
_____
_____
_____

IN CLOSING
"Jesus is fast"

The day after I was reunited with my seven-year-old self and his fascination with the magic of The Lord's Prayer, I went out looking for a book like this one. And I kept on looking for the next seven years. Finally, I realized it hadn't been written yet so I would have to write it myself.

I spent years struggling and assuming that my lack of talent, education and discipline all made writing exceedingly difficult for me; but this was not true. It was trying hard that made it hard. It was in the shower, on long walks, and in the middle of the night when I received most of these insights as gifts. That's how the challenge of fulfilling my own dream gradually revealed that letting go is the key to both a happy life and meaningful and effective prayer.

One afternoon, in Colorado, I was struggling to express an idea when our son Shawn, four-years-old at the time, came rushing into my office. He was extremely excited, and I assumed he'd just completed a new trick on his bike. But to my surprise he said, "Dad I want to be just like Jesus"! All I could think of to say was "why?" Shawn looked at me and proclaimed, "Dad, Jesus is fast". Then before I could respond he bolted out of the room and went back to his bike. I was shocked because Shawn had so simply woven the oath of Peter Pan, Albert Einstein's Theory of Relativity ($E=mc^2$) and our human fascination with speed into the reality of Jesus. Yes, indeed Jesus is fast, and this was the essence of what I had been struggling to write for the past several days.

Peter's oath is to never grow up, and Einstein's theory ($E=mc^2$) both say that beyond the speed of light, time stops. But Jesus knows the fountain of youth and light speed are simply realized as we let go. Jesus knows that "Surfing Love" is how we transcend, and the Lord's Prayer is His invitation to "do even greater things than these". This promise is the one I heard when I was seven, and the one I've spent most of my life pursuing. For me, this book is a miracle made possible by beings like Albert, Jesus, Peter Pan, & Shawn whose simple faith and divine wisdom have given me the permission I needed to let go of my self-imposed limitations and go for it. **Letting go** is the bottom line. Letting go is how each of us surfs the realms of our souls loving awareness within. And we each do this in our own unique ways in order to live the promise of our lives. It doesn't get any clearer than that!

But for those of you who hear Jesus' promise and feel it in your hearts, you are ready for the ease and grace of fulfilling your dreams through this prayer! And there's more....

25. ORACLES

Barbara and I were guided to discover an actual oracle within the Lord's Prayer. We call it "Oracle of the Heart." Our guidance to discover and work with this oracle comes from the ancient Melchizedek Priesthood and working with it has helped open our eyes to the Lord's Prayer in even more exciting new ways. Here we provide you with an opportunity to begin familiarizing yourself with the process of using an oracle. This will help you to experience this book in a profoundly personal way.

So, what do oracles, or the ancient Melchizedek Priesthood have to do with the Lord's Prayer and our relationship with God today? First of all, some of you may not know what an oracle is. It's a divine messenger or message. Angels for example are oracles but the kind of divine messenger that we are talking about here is a system of information that enables us to receive communication directly from God. If this sounds strange or unrealistic to you, we encourage you to keep an open mind, follow the instructions but most importantly listen to your own inner voice. In many ways our use of this book as an oracle is more like a prayer than what most people think of as an oracle.

Like a prayer the clarity and value of an oracle is determined by the intention and integrity of the person using it. And we do not suggest or recommend the use of oracles for the purpose of seeing into the future, nor for obtaining hidden information about others or for divination of any kind. The oracle that we have been guided to create (Oracle of the Heart™) is a way of looking into your own heart for the purpose of realizing how and what you need to let go of. The value of this information is in how it enables each of us to focus our prayers and spiritual exercises for optimum results.

In the bible "lots" were thrown to assist in the making of difficult decisions. By casting lots it was decided whether Joseph or Matthias should be Judas Iscariots' successor in the apostleship (Acts: 1; 15-26). In Proverbs 1 6:33 it says, "The lot is cast into the lap; but the whole decision is of the Lord". And an oracular device, called the Urim & Thummim was used by the ancient Melchizedek Priesthood. Not much is known about this ancient oracle or the priesthood that used it, but experts believe it consisted of a special pair of dice that were held beneath the breast plate of Arron which was worn by the High Priest. We do however know that this Uirm & Thummim was a method of consulting with God (Ex 28: 30, Lv 8: 8, Dt, 33: 8, Ezr 2: 63 Nm 27: 21).

On practically every page of this book we've emphasized how the heart of this prayer and the key to living a happy, productive spiritual life is each person's willingness and ability to surrender our will to Gods will ("Thy Kingdom come, Thy will be done"). From our work with Oracle of the Heart™ we have learned how inviting God to instruct us in our spiritual exercises is extremely rewarding and productive. Once you've completed this book and all its exercises at least once, then we believe that randomly selecting a chapter and using its exercise will benefit you greatly at any given time. Just open to a page and begin. It's like throwing a die or casting lots, allowing spirit to choose what is for your highest good right now. We

know from our own experiences that this works
amazingly well.

NOTES:

_____

_____

_____

_____

_____

_____

_____

_____

_____

_____

_____

_____

_____

_____

_____

_____

_____

_____

_____

_____

_____

_____

_____

_____

26. TEMPLES

When Barbara and I first committed ourselves to this prayer we shared a vision of people using it to honor their own bodies as divine temples. We saw it being shared amongst friends and families in their homes and we saw many homes becoming sacred temples of worship. For the past thirteen years we've been sharing this prayer in our own home and in many others. We've been blessed to participate in the spiritual transformation of families, businesses, churches, and organizations all over this country, but we're just two people. Our dream is that many more may benefit from our work.

We know from our experiences that taking a few minutes a day to say the Lord's prayer in the morning and in the evening can quickly change your life for the better. If you use the spiritual exercises that we offer, we know they will help improve your relationships, your health, your finances, and your perceptions of life in general.

We've learned that the more we invest in this prayer the faster our lives change and that by inviting our friends and family to share this experience with us our lives change even faster. The law is "As we give so shall we receive" and this wonderful uplifting prayer that Jesus gave to all of us, is one of the most precious, loving gifts that we can share with each other.

*For those of you who decide you'd like to share this experience with others we offer you a few suggestions:

INVITATIONS: Invite people personally. And encourage those who havehad this experience to invite people too, but don't push. Spirit is gentle and each group is like a family that grows in its own unique way.

SACRED SPACE: Create a circle of comfortable chairs. Light somecandles, play some soft music. Set the mood for a spiritual experience.

OPENING PRAYER: Always begin by asking your friends to stand andjoin hands for a short opening prayer. What you say is up to you, but we find that it's a good idea to state your intention for the evening to God.

SPIRITUAL EXERCISE: Reading a chapter and doing the exercise could take between twenty minutes to an hour depending on how muchtime you want to spend in prayer. We suggest that you read the evening's spiritual exercise several times but don't push people beyond what they're comfortable with. Three seems to be a suitable number.

THE BREAK: After the Spiritual exercise take a short break so people can stretch and use the bathroom but no more than ten minutes.

SHARING: After the break invite people to share their experiences, their questions and how the prayer is changing their lives. Don't play the role of counselor or pastor just be a loving host and facilitator. To receive from Spirit is the purpose of prayer.

REFRESHMENTS: Simple refreshments are optional but stay focused on the spiritual purpose of your gathering.

DONATIONS: When we give something to people it's important to create an opportunity for them to give something in return. Placing a small basket or bowl in the center of your circle for donations is as much for them as for you. It is giving that enables us to receive and receiving that enables us to give even more.

NOTE: Every individual family or group has its own unique qualities, needs and personality. Once your family or group has gone through this book together, chapter by chapter, you may what to continue working with it as an oracle (see page 111). The collective spiritual energy of a group is quite powerful. So, by working together you will accelerate your personal and spiritual growth.

SPIRITUAL EXERCISE: It's not always possible to share with everyone we would like to but in this holographic universe we are all connected. By simply thinking of the people we love, care about and or are concerned about we may include them in our prayers. Before you begin to pray, call upon their spirits to participate and join you in prayer. As you begin, trust that we are all one body praying for the birth of "Heaven on Earth," or "Gods Kingdom" within all our lives. See yourselves joining together in faith and hope; this or something better for the Highest Good. Do this for a week and observe what happens in the lives of your friends and loved ones, and in your own. Observe how inviting them into your prayers enhances your experience while nurturing your spiritual family.

Baruch Bashan
(The blessings already are)

For More visit us @ seeyourselfloving.com

Or

Oracleoftheheart.com

*"The soul's greatest joy is in discovering itself
and in helping others to achieve the same goal."*

*Paramhansa Yogananda, author of
Autobiography of a Yogi*